# Bass Fishing

## Tips, Techniques, and Strategies for Catching Big Bass

*(Learn the Most Effective Bass Fishing Techniques to Catch Largemouth Bass)*

**Paul Richards**

Published By **Elena Holly**

# Paul Richards

*Bass Fishing: Tips, Techniques, and Strategies for Catching Big Bass (Learn the Most Effective Bass Fishing Techniques to Catch Largemouth Bass)*

## ISBN  978-1-7770736-2-6

No part of this guidebook shall be reproduced in any form without permission in writing from the publisher except in the case of brief quotations embodied in critical articles or reviews.

Legal & Disclaimer

Table Of Contents

## Chapter 1: Bass Blessing

Fishing for bass is a popular hobby for many anglers however, to be able to capture the most powerful and largest catch, it is essential to know the meaning behind the bass blessing. It is a method that requires preparing and maintaining your gear as well as selecting the appropriate fishing lures and baits in order to maximize your fishing success and increase your fishing experience overall.

Preparing and Caring for Your Equipment

The initial step towards achieving getting the bass to bite is properly planning and maintaining your gear. Making sure you are properly preparing and managing your equipment means selecting the best reel and rod for your fishing needs and making sure that the reel is in good working order and properly spooled. It's essential to routinely take care of and clean your equipment and properly store it whenever it's not in use.

Baits and Lures

You should also be aware of the lures and baits you choose to use. Making sure you choose the correct lure or bait for your circumstances, because certain lures and baits work better in different situations. Live bait, for instance is more efficient in calm and clear waters and artificial lures could be more suitable for fishing with murky or stained waters.

Understanding the Behavior and Habits of Bass

An additional aspect to consider in bass fishing is knowing the habits and behavior of bass. The knowledge gained from this can help you determine the most productive locations on bodies of water, and also choose the appropriate baits and lures for your situation. Being aware of the changing seasons for bass as well as the conditions of the weather can help you determine the best places the best time, place and method you should fish.

The importance of respecting and relating to the Natural World

The final point is that bass blessing requires being respectful and in tune with nature and the fishing you capture. It's crucial to know how bass play a role in their natural ecosystem as well as the importance to release them back in the waters responsibly and in a sustainable way. Connecting and respect are not just a way to keep the health and wellbeing of the fish, but will also provide a satisfying fishing experience for you as well as those around you.

If you can master the principles of blessing the bass it will be possible to catch bigger and more fish, and have an exciting and satisfying fishing experience. This is only the first step on your path to learn the art of bass blessing.

The Science of Bass Blessing

In order to truly be a master of fishing for bass It is essential to comprehend the research that drives the process. When you know the nature and behaviour of the bass as well as the environmental aspects that influence the way they feed it will be possible to maximize your fishing success as well as increase the overall performance.

Understanding the Behavior and Feeding Habits of Bass

One of the essential elements in understanding the science behind bass fishing is to understand the habits of feeding and behaviour of bass. Bass are prey fish, which feed on numerous smaller fish as well as aquatic insects. They're active most of the early morning, and in late evening, when the water is less agitated and light levels are lower. Also, they tend to be active more frequently during times with high barometric pressure, and warm months.

The Role of Water Temperature in Bass Behavior

Another important element of research into bass fishing is the understanding of the importance of temperature in the behavior of bass. Bass are cold-blooded, and their metabolism as well as consumption habits are closely linked to the temperature of the water. The general rule is that bass are more active and feed more when the temperature is hotter, whereas they are more inactive and less hungry when the temperature is lower.

The Water Chemistry

The chemistry of the water also is a crucial factor when it comes to bass fishing. The different bodies of water will have distinct water chemistry, and therefore, various forage bases. The information provided here will help you decide which type of lures, baits, or strategies work the best for the specific body of water.

The Role of the Weather Conditions and Tides

The weather conditions as well as tides can play a significant part in the study of fishing for bass. Pressure, direction of the wind and tide levels influence the behavior of bass and their feeding patterns. If you are aware of these variables as well as how they impact bass, you will be able to organize your fishing trips and choose the appropriate equipment and lures that are appropriate for the conditions.

If you are able to understand the science behind bass fishing, it is possible to increase the amount of fish you catch and enhance the overall success of your fishing. These skills, along with the methods and strategies described in the preceding section, will provide you with the skills needed to be an effective and responsible bass fishing enthusiast.

Basics for Bass Fishing

The bass fishing experience is thrilling and well-loved game that is enjoyed by anglers from all over the world. If you want to be an effective bass angler it is essential to understand techniques, equipment and tactics. In this section, we will discuss all the necessary information you'll need for your first angler's journey.

The Fishing Rod and Reel The base of bass fishing starts with choosing the appropriate rod or reel. Pick a medium or moderately heavy spinning rod or a baitcasting rod, based on your preferences and degree. Make sure you choose the right reel, with a smooth drag system, as well as an adequate line capacity.

Fishing Line: Pick the best fishing line available which is suitable for the conditions and the techniques you'll employ. Monofilament, fluorocarbon and braided lines are often used for fishing bass. Monofilament lines can be used for a variety of purposes and are inexpensive, while fluorocarbon lines are almost invisible in the water, while braided lines are extremely strong and sensitivity.

Hooks as well as Terminal Tackle Make sure you have a range of hooks that are suitable for various methods of fishing and bait presentation. The most popular hooks to fish for bass include offset hooks, worm hooks and Treble hooks. In addition, you should stock up on the essential terminal equipment like swings, weights, and snaps for a custom-made presentation and rigs.

Baits and Lures Diverse selection of baits and lures is crucial to entice bass to take a bite. Begin with a variety of options such as soft plastic worms, creatures baits, crankbaits as well as topwater lures. Try various sizes, colors, and movements to suit the current conditions, and to mimic the predatory behavior of the bass.

Tackle Storage: Get bags or tackle boxes for keeping your fishing gear in order and easy to access. Think about a bag with several compartments that can accommodate different kinds of lures and sizes. The lure should also be strong and waterproof to guard your lure from weather and other elements.

Fishing accessories: Many items will enhance your fishing experience. They include sunglasses with polarization to enhance your visibility underwater and a sun hat to provide protection as well as sunscreen and insect repellent, pliers and a multitools for taking hooks off and landing nets to ensure the safety of fish caught, and an instrument to measure tape and a scale to accurately record your catches.

The right attire for fishing is essential to ensure comfort and security while fishing for bass. Pick lightweight, breathable and quick drying clothing appropriate for the current climate. Take into consideration items such as fishing shirts, hats and sunglasses that offer UV protection, footwear that is waterproof as well as a rain jacket to protect yourself from weather conditions.

The safety and navigational equipment Be sure to stay safe when you are on the water with the appropriate equipment. Personal flotation devices (PFD) also known as a life vest is vital. A trusted compass, and GPS device, waterproof map of the area where fishing is permitted as well as a whistle, or air horn to signal as well as a fully powered mobile phone and marine radio are vital for emergency situations and navigation.

Making sure you have the necessary gear is essential for an enjoyable trip to the bass fishing lake. With the correct fishing rods and reels picking the appropriate hooks and lines and stocking up with a variety of baits and lures, organizing your fishing gear and taking into account the safety aspect as well as comfort You will be ready to enjoy the thrilling experience of fishing for bass.

Be sure to keep improving your knowledge and abilities while you progress playing this thrilling sport.

Exploring the Best Baits for Bass Fishing

Picking the correct bait is vital to get bass to take a bite. There are a myriad of options to choose from It is essential to know the various types of baits and their performance in various circumstances of fishing. This article will review some of the top Baits to catch bass and provide information on the characteristics of each and how you can make use of the best ones.

Soft Plastic Worms Soft worms are among the most flexible and powerful baits used for bass fishing. They are available in different dimensions, colors, and shapes. Examples include curly-tail and straight-tail as well as creatures baits. Set them up using a hook for worms, the rig is either Texas-rigged or Carolina-rigged and slowly work them down the bottom or in the vegetation. Soft plastic worms are especially efficient in water that is murky as well as when bass feed on prey that is residing in the bottom.

Crankbaits: These are tough-bodied lures that have an elongated lip or bill which can cause them to dive or move around in the waters. They're made to mimic baitfish, and be used to cover large areas quickly. Pick crankbaits that have different dive depths for diversification of the depths in which you can swim. Try different retrieving speeds as well as stops to imitate wounded prey, and then strike triggers. Crankbaits work well in clear water, near structures as well as during busy feeding times.

Spinnerbaits are made up of an iron blade(s) which rotates when the bait is removed which causes a flash and the sound of. They're great to cover large areas while attracting attention to the bait. Pick spinnerbaits that have various blade sizes and configurations as well as varying the retrieve speed in order to determine the angler's preferred speed. Spinnerbaits work best in water that is murky or stained or around vegetation like fallen trees and in light conditions.

Jigs: Jigs are multi-purpose baits that look like crayfish, baitfish or any other bottom-dwelling animals. They are comprised of an unweighted head along with a skirt as well as trailer (e.g. the soft plastic crawfish, or other creature bait). Jigs can be turned upside down or targeted with specific objects or walked across the bottom or even swam through the plants.

Check that the weight and colors of the jig is appropriate to the clarity and depth of the lake. Jigs can be used all year round and are particularly effective in areas of rock or around submerged structures as well as when bass are not active.

Topwater Lures: These lures produce the appearance of a disturbance on the surface and also mimic injuries to prey to draw bass from beneath. This includes strolling baits, buzzbaits and Frogs. Make use of topwater lures in dim light conditions, particularly in the early morning, as well as in evenings where bass are likely to feed close to the water's surface. Test different retrieves speed, pauses, and tempo in order to replicate different species of predators. Topwater lures can be extremely effective when calm waters are in place, near vegetation, as well as during warm months.

Swimbaits: Swimbaits look like soft plastic lures made to resemble baitfish. They are available in different sizes, ranging from tiny to big, and they can be tied to the jig head, or used as a trailer for chatter or spinner baits. Retrieve swimbaits slowly in order to imitate the swimming of fish.

They're effective when in clear water, close to structures and also in situations where bass eat baitfish.

Picking the right bait to catch bass is based on a variety of factors, such as the conditions of the water, time of day, as well as the patterns of feeding that bass use. Soft plastic worms and crankbaits spinnerbaits, Jigs, topwater lures and swimbaits are every bait that has been proven to assist you in getting bass to strike.

Be sure to test various sizes, colors, and retrieve techniques in order to figure out which one is most effective in certain circumstances. When you understand the qualities and uses of these baits can increase the likelihood of a satisfying angler experience.

Understanding the Best Time for Bass Fishing

The fishing for bass requires excellent ability to judge timing. Finding the right time to catch fish will greatly increase the chances of catching the perfect bass. This article will examine the variables that affect bass behaviour throughout the day, and also the best time frame for success with bass fishing.

Early Morning:

The early morning hours, usually just before sunrise, is as one of the most effective times to fish for bass. The day is ending and the sun sets, bass can be energetic and hungry to feed. In this time it tends to be cooler and it is possible to spot bass nearer to structures or the cover. Topwater lures such as walking baits and poppers, are extremely effective since they mimic injured or struggling prey that is on the surface of the water.

Late Afternoon and Evening:

Like the morning hours, late afternoon and evening are likely to provide an excellent opportunity to fish for bass. After sunset the bass gets more active and feeds on smaller regions. Look for areas that have cover like submerged vegetation, docks, and dead trees as bass might make use of these structures for ambushing predators. Diverse baits are effective at this time and include crankbaits spinnerbaits and soft plastic baits such as worms.

Low-Light Conditions:

Bass generally becomes more active when there is low light like clouds, overcast days or when there is mild rain. This reduces the amount of sunlight reaching the water and make bass feel less secluded and less shaky. Bass might enter water that is shallower or move towards the surface to search for sources of food. In order to attract bass under the conditions described above, you should use lures that cause sound, vibration, or disturbing the surface like spinnerbaits, buzz baits as well as topwater lures.

Seasonal Considerations:

The impact of the seasons on the behaviour of bass is vital to a successful fishing experience. When the bass are in spring, they are in pre-spawn as well as stages of spawning. They move to the shallows near the bed spawning sites. Morning and afternoon is the best time to fish these areas by using lures which mimic baitfish, or mimic defensive behaviour. In summer the bass will seek more shade or deeper waters when it is hot during the day. This can make the fishing in the mornings or at night more successful. When the season turns to fall, bass become more active because they consume a lot of food to prepare for winter. Throughout the day fishing is often successful.

## Chapter 2: Choosing The Right Equipment For Bass Fishing

Finding the best equipment is crucial to a successful bass fishing. No matter if you're an amateur or an experienced professional selecting the correct rod, reel, or line is essential to catch and landing huge bass. In this article we'll take a closer look at choosing the best equipment to meet the needs of your fishing.

Rod

In selecting a rod you must consider the kind of fishing that you'll be taking part in. A lightweight rod that has a quick taper is best when you're fishing small streams or ponds. In contrast when you're fishing big rivers or lakes A medium-action rod that has moderate taper is the best choice. Also, it is important to think about the length of the rod since a rod that is longer can provide you with more range of casting and will allow you to control the angler.

Reel

In selecting a reel you must consider the strength and size of the fish you're aiming for as well as the kind of fishing that you'll do. An asymmetrical reel is more user-friendly and maintenance-free and can be a great option for those who are new to fishing or on smaller bodies of water. In contrast the bait-casting reels are better suited for anglers with experience as well as fishing larger lakes, in which greater power and accuracy are required.

Line

The kind of line you pick is also a significant aspect to take into consideration. A Monofilament line is a sought-after choice for anglers, and works well in all circumstances of fishing. It's cheap, simple to cast and has high sensitivity as well as abrasion resistance. If you're fishing with thick cover, or are using bigger lures, you might want to consider an unbraided or fluorocarbon line with greater power and more sensitiveness.

Other Pieces of Equipment

Apart from the reel, rod along with the line there are other equipment pieces which are essential to a successful fishing experience for bass. This includes a landing net along with pliers, an oar remover and a quality fishing knife. They will assist you in get your catch safely quickly and easily, as well as adjust your gear when you go fishing.

Landing big bass will be much easier when you select the appropriate equipment and are aware of the best way to utilize it. The knowledge you acquire through this experience will assist you to become a more competent and responsible bass fishing guide by combining the information and strategies described in earlier chapters.

Understanding Bait and Lures

Bait and lures play a vital role for bass fishing making the correct choice could make all the difference to the quality of your catch. In this post we'll examine the various types of baits and lures that are available, and also which one for the various conditions you're fishing.

In terms of bait Live bait is usually the ideal option for fishing bass. Live worms and minnows as well as crickets and other tiny creatures are extremely effective at catching bass since they mimic natural sources of food for fish. Baits made of live are most efficient in calm, clear waters where fish can smell and detect they quickly.

Artificial lures such as soft plastic worms, crankbaits and spinnerbaits can be highly effective when it comes to bass fishing. They can be utilized to replicate the appearance and movements of live bait. Additionally, they are a great option for water that is stained or muddy in which fish encounter a harder time viewing live bait.

In selecting a lure, or bait, you need to take into consideration the type of water that you'll be fishing in. For instance, in the clear waters, it's important to choose natural-looking lures like worms and minnows which mimic nature-based food sources for the fish. However when you're in murky or stained water, it's best to select lures that produce lots of sound or vibrating, like spinnerbaits or crankbaits, in order to entice fishing.

A key aspect to consider when selecting an appropriate bait or lure is its size and colour. Baits and lures that have identical in size and hue like the foods of bass are more likely be effective. Also, it is important to be aware of the seasons and the weather, since bass will prefer certain baits or lures, based on conditions of the weather and temperature.

Understanding the different kinds of lures and baits that are available and the best way to choose the best ones for specific circumstances, you'll be more likely to have a better chance of taking on huge bass. Learning about the various kinds of bait and knowing how you can choose the appropriate one, in conjunction with the skills and knowledge described in the preceding chapter, will equip you with all the information you require to be competent and accountable bass fisherman.

## Chapter 3: The Art Of Casting

Casting is a crucial part of bass fishing and mastering how to cast can be a huge difference to the rate of your catch. In this section we'll have a close examine the many casting methods and techniques that will help you increase the accuracy of your casting, distance as well as overall performance.

Having the Right Equipment

In the first place, getting the best casting gear is essential. An excellent rod, and a properly matched reel makes casting simpler and efficient. Also, it is essential to get an appropriate line to what type of fishing that you'll engage in and also to make sure that the line is properly tied and in good shape.

Holding the Rod

The fundamental casting method is to hold the rod using your dominant hand, and then employing your hand to hold the line. When casting, you'll need be able to shift the rod in a back and forth with a fluid and smooth motion, while releasing and holding onto the line using your hand. It is important to ensure that your motions are as fluid and smooth as possible and beware of abrupt or jerky movements.

Maintaining the Proper Form

The most important aspects of casting is the need to keep the correct form. A good casting technique includes:

Maintain your elbow in close proximity towards your body.

Make sure your wrist stays firm and straight.

Use your shoulders and your body to create power.

The correct posture will assist you to cast further and with greater accuracy.

## Practicing Your Casting Techniques

A second important part of casting is the need to hone the casting technique. As you get more practiced the more relaxed and confident you'll feel in your gear and more likely to land huge fishing fish. Training in different situations and conditions is essential to become acquainted with different casting difficulties.

Be aware it is that casting requires a mixture of practice and technique Therefore, you must practice your craft and keep trying out different casting techniques.

When you master how to cast you'll increase your odds of catching large bass. This, along with the techniques and knowledge described in earlier chapters, will provide you with the skills needed to be a responsible and successful bass fishing enthusiast.

Identifying the Best Spots to Fish

One of the key elements of the art of bass fishing success is the ability to scan the waters and determine the most productive locations to catch be fishing. In this article we'll explore how you can identify and snag the most productive spots in the body of water.

This is how you can identify the top spots on the body of water

The Structure

While reading water the structure of the water is among the main things you should be looking for. It includes everything which could provide protection or a habitat for bass such as sandstones and logs, weed bed dropping-offs, and weed beds. These are great locations to catch fish because bass tend to congregate within or around these structures.

## Changes in the Bottom Contour

A further important aspect to read the waters is to search at the changes that occur in the contour of the bottom. The fishing is great also in zones with transition zones between shallow and deep bottoms, or between floors that are soft and hard since these zones provide the perfect fishing zone to fish in transition.

## Current and Tide

Additionally, tide and current are important factors to take into consideration in analyzing the waters. It can be a great way to provide oxygen and food to the fish. Likewise, tides can impact the eating habits of fish as well as the movements of baitfish. Being aware of these elements and the way they impact fish will help you determine which are the top spots for fishing.

Weather and Time of Day

Also, it is important to keep an eye on the weather conditions and time of day in order to pinpoint the most productive spots for fishing. The weather conditions like the direction of wind as well as barometric pressure influence the behavior of fish and the time of the day may influence the way that fish eat. If you are aware of these variables and their impact on the fish and their behavior, you'll be able find the ideal locations to take a fish.

Your chances will increase to catch large fish by gaining the ability to read water and identify the most productive spots for fishing, and be aware of the effects of tide, current as well as the weather and time of the day.

## Chapter 4: Bass Fishing In Different Seasons

Fishing for bass can be an all-year-round sport, however the habits and behavior of bass change through the season. In this article we'll take a deeper review of how changes in the seasons affect the behavior and behavior of bass, and the best way to adapt your fishing strategies accordingly.

Spring

Spring occurs when the temperatures rise in the water, which makes the fish begin to move towards shallower depths of. In this time bass are likely to be feeding continuously and could be caught with a variety of techniques like casting worms made of soft plastic or crankbaits. If the water continues to get warmer in summer months, bass shift to deeper water, and may be caught with techniques like drop-shotting or Jigging.

## Fall

It is during the fall time when the temperatures of the water begin to drop as the fish begin to return to shallower waters. In this time it is likely that bass will be active in eating and may be captured using different methods like casting spinnerbaits and topwater lures. If the water continues to cool in winter months, bass be drawn into deeper waters and may be caught with methods such as slow-rolling spinnerbaits, or jigging soft plastic bait.

## Weather and Water Conditions

It's also important to take into consideration the weather and conditions throughout the various season. In particular, the water gets warmer in the season of spring and summer. Also, bass might be more active. This makes it a great time to catch fish in the daytime. The water, however, is more cool in autumn and winter months as well, which means that bass are more active in the morning and at dusk. This makes it an ideal time to go fishing.

The Water's Forage Base

A further important aspect to take into consideration is the base for the forage of the water body. In different seasons the base forage area in the water body can change so be sure that you adjust the size and kind of baits and lures that you employ according. For instance, in the spring and summer months, where the water temperature is higher and there's more aquatic vegetation, it is possible to choose smaller lures or baits that resemble the size of the forage. But, if the water temperature is cooler, and the base of forage differs between winter and the fall it is possible to utilize larger lures and baits.

Understanding the behaviour and patterns of bass all through the year, and adapting the techniques you use to catch bass to enhance your chances of catching large bass and becoming an experienced and responsible bass angler.

Responsible and Sustainable Ethics Bass Fishing

Fishing for bass can be satisfying and fun, but it's crucial to consider the significance of conservation and ethical standards. In this article we'll take a closer look at ways to be eco-friendly and sustainable as well as the benefits.

The first step towards conservation is to learn and comply with the guidelines established by state officials. Being aware of and following the rules can mean limiting the quantity and size of fish you can capture and the types of gear. It is not only vital to observe these rules However, it's crucial to know the logic of them as well as the ways they can help protect the population of fish.

Another crucial aspect of conserving is practicing catch-and release fishing. Catch-and release is a method that allows you to catch a fish, and return it in a healthy condition back to the waters. By practicing catch-and release, fish are able to reproduce and grow and help maintain healthy populations of fish.

If you are doing catch and release it is crucial to manage the fish in a safe manner and make use of barbless hooks or get rid of the hooks as swiftly and as safely as is possible in order so as to minimize the pressure on the fish.

Also, it's important to pay attention to the effects on the environment as well as the impacts on the environment from fishing. Becoming aware of the impact on the environment is not littering or destroying the habitats of fish. It is important to use fishing zones that have been designated and to avoid disturbing habitats that are sensitive like spawning zones or habitats that support other animals.

When you are a sustainable and ethical angler, you'll not just help protect ecosystem and fish populations and the environment, but also providing a satisfying fishing experience for both you and the people who are around you. Together with the skills and knowledge outlined in the previous chapters, will provide you with the necessary tools to succeed as a accountable bass fisherman.

## Chapter 5: Catching And Releasing

Releasing and fishing is essential to the responsible and sustainable bass fishing. When you release the fish without harm it will help ensure healthy populations of fish as well as ensure the sustainability for this sport. In this section we'll have a more detailed review of the significance to catch and release, as well as how to make sure you are able to guarantee that you have a safe and proper release of the bass.

Regulations

The first step for catch-and-release fishing is understanding the rules and regulations imposed by state authorities. Numerous states have implemented catch and release rules specific to certain species of fish, for example, bass in order to protect populations of fish. It is vital to be aware of and adhere to these rules, and also to comprehend the reasons behind them as well as the ways they can help protect the population of fish.

Equipment

After you have a clear understanding of how to use the rules, having the suitable equipment to catch and release fish is crucial. The process involves barbless hooks, or taking away the hooks in a safe and speedy manner so as to lessen the strain for the fish. Also, it is essential to make use of the correct landing nets and techniques in order to cut down on handling time and to avoid injuries on the fishing species.

Handling the Fish

The fish should be handled gently and with care when you catch the bass and then releasing it is crucial. The proper handling of the fish involves making sure that the fish is within the water for as long as you can and using damp hands while holding the fish. Also, it is important to hold the weight of the fish by holding it in a horizontal position instead of vertically in order to reduce stress and injury on the fish.

Releasing the Fish

It's equally important to let the fish go as quickly and as safely as you can and make sure it is able to swim away with a lot of force prior to release. You must avoid release of the fish in places which it might not be able to survive for long, like shallow water or under the sun.

Understanding the importance to catch and release as well as using the most effective techniques, you can to maintain healthy populations of fish and secure a long-term development for the bass fishing industry. This chapter, along with the information and methods that were discussed in earlier chapters will equip you with the necessary tools to become a responsible, sustainable bass angler.

The Role of Weather and Tides in Bass Fishing

Tide and weather have a huge impact on the fishing of bass, and knowing how these elements influence the behaviour and habits of bass may help you gain an advantage while fishing. In this part we'll take a deeper study of the significance of the weather and tides on bass fishing and ways that you can utilize this information to increase the amount of fish you catch.

Water Temperature

One of the main things to be aware of in the context of weather is the temperature of the water. If the water temperature changes as do the behaviors and behavior of bass. In particular, in the season of spring and summer as the water becomes warmer, bass are more active. They can be caught by using a variety of methods, like casting worms made of soft plastic or crankbaits.

In contrast in the winter and fall seasons as the water becomes cooler, bass tend to become less active, and can be caught with techniques like slow-rolling a spinner bait or jigging with a soft plastic lure.

Barometric Pressure

Another important factor to think about in relation to weather is barometric pressure. Pressure can influence the behaviour of bass and pressure changes can indicate a change in temperature. Bass might be more active in times that are high pressure, and lower in activity during periods that are low pressure.

Tides

Tides also play a major influence on bass fishing especially in areas along the coast in which the level of water can alter drastically.

## Chapter 6: Understanding Bass Biology And Ecology

Learning about the biology and ecology of bass can allow you connect to the fish that you catch, and to appreciate their importance within the ecological system. In this article we'll take a deeper review of the ecology and biology of bass. We'll also discuss how the knowledge gained can assist you become a more mindful and considerate fishing enthusiast.

Bass is also known as Micropterus which is a freshwater fish that is native in North America. These fish are warm water and are found in a diverse range of habitats including lakes, rivers as well as reservoirs. They can be predators that are open to taking on a variety of prey species, which include crustaceans, insects and even smaller fish.

Bass are known for their complicated life-cycle, that involves a spawning phase during the summer and spring. At this time it is common for the fish to be drawn into deeper water to spawn. It is essential to keep a safe distance from these areas in order to ensure the fish as well as their offspring.

Numerous factors can impact Bass population, such as environmental factors, habitat destruction as well as overfishing. For a responsible fishing angler It is crucial to know these aspects and do everything to help protect the environment and fish. Knowing these aspects includes:

Training in Catch and Release fishing.

Avoid excessive fishing.

Be aware of the negative impact that fishing has on the natural environment.

When you understand the ecology and biology of bass, you will be able to be able to connect with them at a higher level and be aware of their importance to the ecology. It can also assist to become a considerate and ethical fisherman, taking care of the environment and fish. Always be aware of the negative impact fishing has on the surrounding environment and be respectful to the fish.

Advanced Bass Fishing Techniques

Modern bass fishing techniques will assist you to increase your rate of catch as well as focus on certain types of bass. In this article we'll discuss the most advanced methods, like trolling or jigging, as well as methods to employ these techniques to capture bass.

Trolling

Trolling is an approach that allows anglers to use the boat to gradually move across the lake as they cast or drag lures along behind. Trolling lets anglers take advantage of a vast area of water, and also target particular species of bass like largemouth and smallmouth bass.

Trolling is commonly used for fishing on open waters for example, lakes or reservoirs. It is a great way to take bass caught within the column of water. In order to troll effectively be aware at the rate of your vessel, the depth of your lures, and also the lures that you choose to use.

Jigging

Jigging is a different method that can be used to catch certain types of bass. Jigging is the use of a jig which is a kind of lure that has a head weighted as well as a soft plastic tail that mimics the movement from live fish. Jigging is typically used when fishing deeper waters or in areas around structures like logs, rocks, or grass bed. For a successful jigging experience it is important to take note of the depth of water, the style of jig used and also the speed at which you retrieve.

Jigging and trolling can work well to catch bass, however, you need to be sure to only employ them under conditions that are suitable and using appropriate equipment. It is important to be aware of the condition of the water, the structures and type of fish you intend to target before deciding the appropriate method. Trolling is effective in deeper as well as open water, whereas Jigging can be more efficient in water that is shallow and has the structure.

If you can master these methods, you will improve your odds of landing big catch of fish. Be aware of the environment along with the shape and nature of the fish that you are choosing the right method.

## Chapter 7: The Mental And Emotional Aspects Of Bass Fishing

The sport of fishing for bass is an sport that involves physical effort and includes emotional and mental components which can greatly impact the experience of fishing. In this section we'll discuss how you can tackle the emotional and mental aspects of fishing for bass and enhance the fishing experience.

The aspect of mentality in bass fishing is maintaining the proper mental attitude and mindset when you are fishing. Being in the right mindset and attitude is being tolerant as well as focused and capable of adapting to changes in circumstances. It's essential to think positively about fishing and open to learning different techniques and trying out various techniques. A positive outlook while fishing, regardless of whether it's slow fishing will help you maximize the chances of fishing.

The psychological part of fishing for bass is tightly linked to the mental aspect. Fishing can be a very emotion-filled experience that brings pleasure, happiness and tranquility. It's important to make time to take in nature's splendor and to be aware of being present in the moment. Fishing is a wonderful opportunity to get away from pressures and replenish your energy.

Another way to boost the mental and emotional aspect is to go fishing with your friends or your family. The experience of fishing with other people can foster an atmosphere of camaraderie and sharing experiences create memories that last a life time. Also, it can be an ideal opportunity to instruct kids or newcomers to how to fish and share the passion for fishing.

Another approach to creating more enjoyable and satisfying fishing experiences is to integrate mindfulness techniques including meditation, or yoga in your daily fishing routine. They can assist to lessen anxiety and stress, as well as improve focus and concentration.

If you can approach the emotional and mental aspects of fishing for bass with an attitude and mindset that is right You can have an enjoyable and satisfying fishing experience, while also giving you the necessary tools to succeed as a competent bass angler.

Techniques Strategies, Tips and Tricks to fishing with Lures

Lures are an essential part of bass fishing. Picking the appropriate lure for the appropriate situation will greatly improve your chance of catching the fish. In this article we'll have a deeper examine different kinds of lures, techniques and techniques to utilize to make them more effective, as well as the techniques that can make them more efficient.

Soft Plastic Worms

A very well-known varieties of bass fishing lures fishing are soft plastic Worms. These lures can be used in a variety of ways and are able to be utilized for a wide variety of scenarios including casting and flipping. They can be fished with various rigs like the Texas Rig or an Carolina Rig, or an unusual rig. It is effective in the capture of large and smallmouth bass. For the best results from soft plastic worms, is essential that you pay attention to the dimensions and colors of the worm and also the kind of fishing rig you're fishing with.

Crankbaits

Another type of lure popular used for fishing bass is crankbaits. They are made to imitate the appearance and movements of smaller fish and may be utilized to hunt for bass active eating. Fishing crankbaits can be done using a variety of retrieves including medium, slow or speed as well as capture largemouth and smallmouth bass. Be aware of the dimensions, colors and speed of the crankbait for the best results. the most out of the baits.

Topwater Lures

Another type of lure used for bass fishing is the topwater lures. They are made to imitate the look and movements of insects as well as tiny fish that are floating on the water's surface, and are able to target bass that feed on the top of the water. Topwater lures can be fished with different retrieves like walking your dog, or popping. They will catch both smallmouth and largemouth bass.

Apart from being aware of the size of the lure, its color and retrieve that the lure is used topwater lures need to be properly retrieved.

Another trick to consider when fishing with lures is to change the lure's presentation. The fish can get used to certain lures or presentation, therefore changing the lure's appearance and design is essential to keep them guessing. Change your color, size the lure's type, and even the rig that you employ.

A different trick to use when fishing with lures is to employ the trailer hook. The trailer hook is a tiny hook that is attached to the rear of the lure. it increases the chance of hooking fish simply nicking at the lure. This is especially useful in the case of soft plastic worms and different plastic lures.

## Chapter 8: Bass Fishing Tournaments

Fishing tournaments in bass provide a wonderful opportunity to practice your fishing skills and to compete with other anglers. In this article we'll have a more detailed review of how you can prepare for and participate in bass fishing tournaments, and the best ways to boost your chances of winning.

The initial step to prepare for a fishing tournament with bass is to become familiar to the regulations and rules for the competition. Knowing the rules and regulations involves being aware of the format for tournaments as well as the limits of the fishing zone as well as the regulations for the use of lures, baits and vessels. Knowing the scoring system as well as punishments for violating the rules are also crucial.

The next step to prepare for an event is to investigate the area of water in which the tournament will take place. The research process involves studying maps, analyzing forecasts for weather, as well as scouting the fishery areas. If you know the conditions of the water and how fish behave and behaviour, you'll be able to take strategic choices when you're competing.

A crucial aspect to consider when preparing for a tournament is making sure the equipment you use is in operating condition. Making sure your equipment is well-maintained includes the inspection of your reels, rods and baits, along with the safety equipment on your boat. It's also beneficial to have extra equipment on hand including spare parts or tools for an eventual situation of emergency.

Keeping your focus and an optimistic mindset is crucial for a successful tournament. Being focused and keeping the right mindset is about staying at ease under pressure, taking smart decisions and adapting to changes in the environment. It is also crucial to keep the mental and physical ability to stay focused during the entire tournament.

If you are aware of the rules, regulations and structure, conducting the necessary research, making sure you have prepared your equipment and keeping an attitude of positivity will help you prepare to participate in a tournament for bass fishing. Be sure to remain focused and make smart decisions and adjust to changes in the conditions throughout the tournament to enhance your odds of success.

Bass Fishing Using Artificial Lures

Artificial lures are an extremely popular and efficient method of catching bass. But picking the correct lure and applying the right methods could make the biggest impact. In this article we'll take a look at diverse kinds of artificial lures, techniques and suggestions to employ them, and the best ways to boost your chances of getting the most out of them.

Soft plasticworms can be among of the most sought-after artificial lures to catch bass. It is possible to use these flexible lures for various scenarios including casting and flipping. Additionally, you could use them with multiple types of rigs like an Texas Rig or the Carolina Rig, or the wacky rig. they're effective in fishing for large and smallmouth bass. Be aware of the color, size and kind of rig you're employing when fishing with soft plastic Worms.

A different type of lure that is popular to catch bass is the crankbait. They are made to imitate the look and motion of small fish, and are able to catch bass engaged in eating. Fishing crankbaits can be done with different retrieves like slow, medium or rapid they are effective in catching largemouth or smallmouth bass.

In order to get the most from crankbaits, take note of the dimensions and shade of the lure, as well as the method of retrieval you choose to use.

Another type of lure used for bass fishing is the topwater lures. These lures are created to imitate the look and movements of insects as well as tiny fish that are floating in the water's surface. They will target bass fishing at the surface of the water. Fishing topwater lures using a variety of retrieves, for example, walking the dog or popping. These lures will catch both smallmouth and largemouth bass. It is essential to know the way topwater lures function in terms of their size and colors to make the most of them.

Also, remember that bass only occasionally active feeding during those times and a more finesse strategy is an excellent idea (this involves employing smaller lures, and thinner lines) as well as slowing the speed of your retrieve. Methods like drop-shotting, shakey-heading, and Ned rigging are effective.

A second tip to use synthetic lures, is to alter your presentation. The fish can get used to a certain lure or display. Therefore, altering your presentation and lure is essential to keep fishing species in the dark. This can be done by altering the color, size as well as the type of lure as well as the retrieve or rig that you use.

## Chapter 9: Bass Fishing With Live Bait

The use of live baits can be an effective strategy to capture bass. In this article we'll have a close examine the different kinds of live baits, their methods and techniques to utilize the bait, as well as how you can enhance your chances of getting the most out of them.

The Different Types of Live Baits

Below are three principal categories of live-baits to use for fishing bass:

Minnows

Minnows are among the most sought-after varieties of live baits used to use for fishing bass. Minnows are a great bait to fish using a variety of rigs like a split-shot the rig, slip-sinker as well as a float device, which will catch smallmouth as well as largemouth bass. For the best results from minnows, it is important to be aware of the size and colour of the minnow, as well as the type of rig that you use.

Worms

Another well-known live bait used for bass fishing are Worms. Fishing with worms is possible. Worms with various rigs like the Texas rod as well as the Carolina one, or drop-shot rigs, and will catch smallmouth as well as largemouth bass. If you are fishing with worms taking note of the size, color as well as the type of rig used is vital.

Crayfish

The third live bait used for bass fishing is the crayfish. Crayfish are able to be caught using different rigs like the jig-rig, a drop-shot rig, or even a flotation rig. These rigs will catch smallmouth as well as largemouth bass. What kind of rig you choose to use along with the size and colour of the crayfish are essential to get the best enjoyment from fishing for crayfish.

Tips and Techniques for Using Live Baits

Fishing with live bait, being attentive to the condition of the water as well as the behavior of fish is crucial. Live bait is typically used bait if the fish aren't actively feeding. Hence, employing a finesse method employing smaller baits, light lines, as well as slowing your retrieve down is vital.

Another suggestion when you are employing Live bait, is that you make sure that the color and size of the bait with the size and hue of the prey that is natural on the lake. By comparing the size and colors could increase the chance of a bass biting.

Another tip when you are using live bait is changing the size, shape and the position of the hook bait in order to increase the appeal to the fish.

A further important element of employing live bait is to keep the bait in good condition and fresh. This means placing it in a living tank or in an aerated one and changing the water regularly. Also, it is essential to choose the right bait for the circumstances, like nightcrawlers with water that is muddy as well as minnows that are clear in water.

Fishing with live bait, being attentive to the tides and fishing at the right times for the tide, like the coming or outgoing tide is vital. This can dramatically increase your chances of landing fish.

If you can master the strategies of tips and tricks that you can use live bait you will increase the chances of landing big fish, and provide a more satisfying fishing experience. Always keep an eye on conditions of the waters, behaviour of the fish, as well as the size and color of the bait. You can be a competent and dependable bass fisherman by using the correct methods, live bait and a proper approach.

Bass Fishing in Different Body of Water

Bass fishing can be done across a variety of bodies of water that include freshwater, saltwater and brackish waters. Every type of water has distinct challenges, and require various strategies and techniques. This article will review the different techniques and tricks to catch bass in saltwater, freshwater and brackish waters.

Freshwater

Freshwater fishing is by far the most popular kind of bass fishing that can be found in rivers, lakes, and streams. Most popular methods to fish freshwater are trolling, casting, and fishing jigging. While fishing in freshwater keeping an eye on the water temperatures, oxygen levels and the food supply for fish is vital.

Additionally, be aware of the weather conditions, and catch fish at the right time of day, for example early in the morning or late at night.

Saltwater

Saltwater fishing should be conducted in bays, estuaries as well as in coastal waters. Most popular methods to fish saltwater include trolling, casting and fishing jigging. If you are fishing in saltwater being aware of the conditions of the tide and fishing at ideal times, like either the outgoing or incoming tide is vital. Additionally, keep an eye on temperatures in the water as well as the salinity level as well as the availability of food for fish.

Brackish Water

Brackish water is a mixture of freshwater and salt, usually found in estuaries or the river mouths. Most popular methods to fish in brackish waters comprise trolling, casting and Jigging. In salty waters it is important to pay attention to conditions of the tide and fishing at most optimal times, for instance either the outgoing or incoming tide is crucial. Also, it is important to be aware of temperatures in the water along with salinity levels as well as the availability of food for fish.

When you master the strategies and tricks for fishing bass using freshwater, saltwater or brackish water, it is possible to enhance your chances of landing big fish, and provide an enjoyable fishing experience. Be sure to be aware of the condition of the water, fishing behavior of the fish and available food.

## Chapter 10: Next Level Bass Fishing

Being a professional bass fisherman Perhaps you're looking at taking your fishing skills to the higher step. In this article we'll discuss the most advanced methods for catching bass that anglers are required to know or learn. These methods can assist you to capture larger fish and provide the most enjoyable fishing experience.

Using a Drop-shot Rig

An innovative method for fishing for bass is to use an rig that drops shots. It's a variant of the split-shot design that allows you to show the bait in a more natural manner. It is particularly useful for the capture of fish with a temperament that is not feeding. The drop-shot rig is comprised of a hook that is attached to the aft end of the line. There is an attached small sinker about a few inches higher than the hook. The bait is then slid on the hook, leaving the hook's edge exposed..

Using a Swimbait

A more sophisticated method of catching bass is to use a swimbait. It is a big soft-bodied lure that is created to emulate the appearance of a live baitfish and its movements. It is possible to fish with swimbaits using a variety of rigs, including a jighead or hook with a weight, and are able to catch largemouth and smallmouth bass.

Using a Jerkbait

A different technique that is more advanced is to use the jerk bait. Jerk bait is a tough-bodied lure made to emulate an actual live baitfish's appearance as well as movements. It is possible to fish an jerk bait on a variety of methods, like the steady or one-handed retrieve. It is able to efficiently catch large and smallmouth bass.

Using a Finesse Approach

A different technique that is more advanced is to use the finesse method. This means that you use lighter lures with smaller sizes as well as slowing down your retrieval. Methods like drop-shotting, shaking-head and Ned method of rigging are effective.

Using a Spinnerbait

A more sophisticated method of catching bass is to use a spinner bait. Spinnerbaits include lures that have metal blades, or blades that spin while the lure moves. The spin of the blades generates flashes and vibrations which can draw bass towards the lure. Spinnerbaits can be fished with diverse retrieves like either a slow or steady retrieve. They can be used to effectively capture largemouth and smallmouth bass. Take note of the color, size and style of blades that be able to match the environment and species you're targeting.

Using a Chatterbait

A different technique that is more advanced is to use the Chatterbait. Chatterbaits resemble Spinnerbaits, but they have the jig's head is a blade rather than a steel blade. They make a distinct vibrating sound that could draw bass. Chatterbaits can be fished using diverse retrieves like either a slow or steady retrieve. They are able to take largemouth and smallmouth bass.

By using the Topwater lure with a Walking-TheDog Retrieve

One of the most advanced techniques you can apply at night involves an upperwater lure that has the walking-the-dog retrieve. The method involves dragging the rod's tip forward and back while reeling the lure in and causing it to move up and down over the water's surface. This can be an effective method to catch bass that feed on topwater during the late at night.

Take note of the size, color, and the type of lure you choose to suit to the environment and fish that you want to catch.

Using a Frog Lure

A different method that is more advanced is to use the Frog Lure. Frog lures are made to mimic the look and movements of a living Frog. It is possible to fish with the frog lure in a variety of types of retrieves, including the regular or a hopping which can catch largemouth and smallmouth bass.

## Chapter 11: Exploring Bass Types, Power, And Distinctions

The bass fishing community is often confronted with different species of bass in their fishing excursions. This article provides provide the basics of various types of bass and explore the causes for their power, and explain the difference between "bass" as well as "bass fishing."

Types of Bass

Largemouth Bass (Micropterus salmoides) Largemouth Bass (Micropterus salmoides) is among the most sought-after and famous species. Largemouth bass live in North America's reservoirs, lakes rivers, ponds, and lakes and are well-known by their huge mouths as well as their an aggressive personality. The largemouth bass can grow to incredible dimensions and are widely sought-after by anglers because of their intense battles and challenging behaviour.

Smallmouth Bass (Micropterus dolomieu) Smallmouth Bass (also known as "smallies," are another well-known species of bass for anglers. Smallmouth bass have smaller mouths, and are well-known by their bronze-colored coloring as well as fierce, athletic combats. Smallmouth bass are a favorite of clean, cool water including streams, rivers and rocky lakes throughout North America and parts of Canada.

Spotted Bass (Micropterus punctulatus) Spotted bass is a close relative of smallmouth and largemouth bass, having similar traits. The majority of them are found in the southeast of the United States and are known for their distinctive rows black spots that line their body. Spotted bass can be aggressive and provide an exciting fishing experience.

Guadalupe Bass (Micropterus triculii) A. The Guadalupe bass is indigenous to the streams and rivers of Texas especially within the Guadalupe River basin. It has a brownish green color with vertical bars. They are smaller than smallmouth and largemouth bass. Guadalupe bass offers a distinctive anglers with the opportunity to fish within their home range.

Why is Bass So Powerful?

Muscular structure: Bass possesses a powerful and muscular body regardless of their species. Strong muscles, particularly those in their tails that are broad, permit them to create fast and explosive speed bursts, as well as do acrobatic leaps once hooked. The muscular characteristics of these fish contribute to the formidable fight ability of bass.

The predatory nature of bass is that they are considered to be apex predators of their environment. They're opportunistic eaters, and have developed the ability to quickly hunt and capture prey. The predatory nature of them is evident in their speed and strength which allows them to dominate and subdue prey.

The burst of energy that occurs when hooked, bass tap an energy reserve, creating a burst of strength and determination. They use their muscle bodies and utilize tactics, such as diving under cover, executing rapid runs and jumping into the water trying to escape the line of an angler.

Difference Between Bass and Bass Fish

Terminology: The word "bass" is often employed to describe the different fish species that belong to the family of Centrarchidae which is also known as the black bass. The family comprises smallmouth bass, largemouth bass, and spotted bass as well as other species closely related to it. However, "bass fish" is the less specific term applied to all fish belonging to the larger bass category.

Generalization: Though "bass" generally refers to a particular species of the Centrarchidae family, "bass fish" is commonly used as a generic term of any fish having similar traits, like an extended physique, flippy fins and predatory characteristics. It could also refer to diverse species belonging to various families, which includes other species that are not considered bass, such as the striped sea bass.

Knowing the various types of bass and their strong nature and distinction of "bass" as well as "bass fish" will enrich your understanding as an enthusiast for bass fishing.

## Chapter 12: Identifying Bass And Understanding Their Habits

Being able to identify bass with accuracy and knowing the behavior of these fish is vital to success in bass fishing. In this chapter, we will provide details on how to identify bass, including physical attributes, as well as the elements that influence their size as well as the depth they prefer to of fishing.

Identifying Bass

Physical Characteristics: All species of bass including smallmouth bass, largemouth bass and spotted bass share some common physical characteristics.

Body Form: Bass has a streamlined shape, that has a laterally compressed shape. They have a big mouth as well as a large tail with a mixture of soft-rayed and spiny fins.

Coloration: The coloring of bass varies based on the environmental conditions, however generally, they show the shades of brown, green or bronze in their backs. They can also be seen changing to lighter shades around their belly and sides. There are also distinctive patterns like black spots or dark vertical bars.

The size of bass size can be different based on the nature of the species and circumstances. Bass that are small and largemouth may over 20 inches and weigh up to several pounds and spotted bass are likely to be a bit smaller.

How Big is the Longest Bass?

It is the World Record: The longest recorded bass ever caught is the world record for largemouth bass that was caught by George Perry in Montgomery Lake, Georgia, USA, in 1932. Perry's bass was 32.5 inches long, and weighted a whopping 22 pounds and 4 grams. The astonishing catch is an eminent achievement when it comes to bass fishing.

Trophy Bass: Though it's not common to catch bass with this size but anglers still have the opportunity to target big bass with their fishing pursuits. They generally go over the size average and are sought-after by anglers looking for a memorable catch. The location of the fish and the species, a trophy bass may weigh between up to 12 pounds.

What Depth do you Fish for Bass?

The bass's preferences for depth are diverse. Bass can be observed at varying depths all through the year dependent on the temperature of the water as well as the availability of prey and the patterns of the seasons. Being aware of their preferred depths will help anglers target bass

Shallow water: During spring and summer months when bass are most active, they move towards shallow waters in order to feed and spawn. They may be seen near areas of shoreline vegetation, submerged plants as well as structures in waters ranging in depth from a couple of inches to several feet.

Mid-Depth range: As season progresses and the water temperatures increase, bass could shift into mid-depth zones. Mid-depth ranges can encompass the depth of 5-15 feet. Here they search for cooler water, and then follow their prey, such as baitfish or the crayfish.

Deep Water The summer heat or in colder months bass might move to deeper waters. Deep water could comprise depths ranging from 15 to 30 feet, or even more, using thermoclines dropping-offs, submerged structures or drop-offs. Deep-water fishing methods including jigging and deep-diving crankbaits can be used to effectively catch bass in these regions.

Aftidating to the Conditions Note that bass behaviour and depths may differ based on the clarity of water as well as weather patterns and the availability of forage. Adjusting to the conditions, by using depthfinders or fish finders may assist anglers to locate bass in the depth they prefer.

The ability to identify bass accurately on the basis of their physical attributes and recognizing their favorite depths to feed as well as habitat is essential for success in bass fishing.

## Chapter 13: Timing And Techniques For Bass Fishing Success

Timing is an essential factor when it comes to fishing for bass. Knowing when and how to capture bass is vital to maximize your odds of getting it right. In this chapter, we will explore the best timing to go bass fishing all year round as well as explore the fascinating subject of the bass's vision, as well as the ability of bass to see even when it is dark.

When to Catch Bass

The bass's preferences for depth are diverse. Bass can be seen at different depths all through the year dependent on the temperature of the water or the available prey species, as well as variations in the season. Being aware of their preferred depths will help anglers target bass

Shallow water: During spring and the early summer it is common for bass to move towards shallow water in order for spawning and feeding. They are often found close to areas of shoreline vegetation, submerged plants as well as structures in the depths of water ranging between a few inches and just a couple of feet.

Mid-Depth range: As summer gets underway and temperatures increase, bass could shift into mid-depth areas. The mid-depth range could include the depth of 5-15 feet. They are looking for cooler waters, and then follow their prey, such as baitfish or the crayfish.

## Chapter 14: Understanding Fresh Water Fishing

Types and definitions of freshwater fishing

Freshwater fishing is a very popular activity for a lot of outdoor enthusiasts. It is about catching fish in lakes, rivers, and streams that have freshwater. There are many kinds of freshwater fishing available, and every one of them requires different methods and gear. In this chapter we'll provide an outline of nature and the types of fishing in freshwater.

Definition of Freshwater Fishing

Freshwater fishing is a form of fishing in water bodies which have less than 0.5 per cent salt amount. The bodies of water that are considered to be freshwater comprise lakes, rivers, ponds and streams. Freshwater fishing differs from saltwater fishing which occurs in oceans seas and various saltwater bodies.

Types of Freshwater Fishing

1. Fly Fishing

The fly fishing method is one type of fishing in freshwater that entails employing a small lure, called an 'fly' to capture fish. It is constructed out of fur, feathers, as well as other substances that are designed to resemble insects as well as other tiny animals that fish eat. Fishing for fly requires special equipment such as the fly rod, reel as well as a line.

2. Spin Fishing

Spin fishing is one of the forms of freshwater fishing which involves using a spinning rod or reel that casts an lure or bait in the waters. The sport is known to catch a wide variety of freshwater fish, such as trout, bass, and panfish. Baits and lures for spin fishing are available in a variety of sizes and form, and may be constructed of metal, plastic, or other natural substances like minnows and worms.

## 3. Baitcasting

Baitcasting refers to a form of freshwater fishing identical to spin fishing however, it needs a distinct kind of rod and reel. Baitcasting reels are made to take on heavier lures and lines and provide greater precision and control while casting. Baitcasting is a popular method of catching large freshwater species, such as pike, musky and catfish.

## 4. Ice Fishing

Ice fishing is one of the types of freshwater fishing which is carried out in frozen water bodies. Ice fishermen make use of special equipment, such as fishing rods, ice augers as well as shelters to capture fish by capturing holes cut in the frozen. Fishing with ice is common in cooler environments and usually connected with the catch of species like perch, walleye as well as northern pike.

Freshwater fishing is a great options to take pleasure in the outdoors, while also catching fish. If you're interested in spinning fishing, fly fishing, baitcasting or the ice fishing method, there's an option of freshwater fishing which will meet your needs and level of skill. If you're a novice is essential to begin at the beginning and slowly move up to more sophisticated methods and equipment. Through practice and perseverance eventually, you'll be catching fish as a professional.

Fish species that live in fresh water

Freshwater fish species are numerous interesting, and are found in an array of places around the globe. If you're a novice fisherman must be aware of the various varieties of freshwater fish might be found on fishing excursions.

The most well-known freshwater species of fish is largemouth bass. The fish is known by its fierce behaviour and fighting skills which makes it a popular choice by anglers. Largemouth bass typically live in weedy, warm waters which can be caught by using various lures and methods.

A freshwater fish species that is also popular is rainbow trout. They are usually found in clear, cold rivers and streams, and they are prized due to their tasty meat. Rainbow trout are caught with a range of lures and baits, such as spinners, live bait and fly flies.

The other freshwater species that are popular are crappie, catfish bluegill, and the walleye. Each one of them is unique in its characteristic and behavior and are caught with many different methods and lures.

In the case of fishing for freshwater species of fish It is important to know the restrictions and regulations for each species that you can find in your region. There are many states that have guidelines regarding limit of catch as well as size limitations as well as fishing seasons. So you should be familiar with the rules before you head out to sea.

In the end, fishing in freshwater is an excellent option to spend time outdoors while experiencing the excitement of catching many species of fish. If you are aware of the various types of freshwater fish, as well as methods for catching these fish, you'll enhance your chances of an enjoyable and successful fishing experience.

Equipment and fishing gear

Equipment and fishing gear are a must for every beginner fishing enthusiast. The tools you use will help you to catch fish, and makes your fishing trip enjoyable. When you fish in a lake, river or pond, you must have the appropriate gear for an enjoyable fishing experience. In this chapter this chapter, we'll go over the diverse types of fishing equipment and other equipment that you'll require as a new angler.

Fishing Rods:

The fishing rod is among the primary tool is required to go fishing. It is vital to pick the rod best suited to the kind of fish you want to capture. Rods for fishing are classified based on dimensions, weight, and their strength. The longer rods are perfect for fishing larger lakes, whereas smaller rods are ideal for smaller streams.

Fishing Reels:

The fishing reel is essential as they assist you reel into your catch. There are three kinds of reels available: spinning, baitcasting reels, as well as spincast reels. The spinning reels are easiest to work with and perfect for novices. Baitcasting reels are more sophisticated and require more expertise in order to effectively use. Spincast reels comprise of spinning and baitcasting reels. They're also great for novices.

Hooks:

Hooks are available in a variety of dimensions and shapes. selecting the proper size of hook is dependent on the kind of fish you wish to capture. The smaller hooks work best for fish that are smaller, and larger hooks are perfect for larger fish. Hooks come in various forms, like J-hooks, circle hooks and Treble hooks.

Fishing Line:

Lines for fishing are essential as they aid in catching fish. There are two kinds of lines used for fishing that are braided and monofilament. Monofilament lines are great for those who are new to fishing as they're easily handled. Lines with braids are more sophisticated and best to experienced anglers.

Bait:

Bait attracts fish to the hook. There are two kinds of baits: live bait as well as artificial bait. Live bait is comprised of worms, crickets and minnows as artificial bait is made up of lures and Flies. Picking the correct bait will depend on the kind of fish you wish to capture.

**Chapter 15: Finding The Right Fishing Spot**

Selecting the best site

Finding the best location is among the main factors to consider in the success of freshwater fishing. No matter if you're a beginner or a seasoned angler picking the ideal spot can be the difference between an enjoyable day of fishing and unsatisfactory results.

The most crucial thing to think about before deciding on a spot is the kind of fish you want to catch. Fish species vary and are attracted to various types of water and environments Therefore, it's crucial to determine which locations will yield the best catch. In particular, bass tend to cluster in areas around the fallen tree and rock While trout are more suited to cool, clear waters.

Another crucial aspect to think about is time of the day. Different species of fish are active at certain times of the day. Therefore, it's important for you to schedule your fishing excursion in accordance with the time of day. As an example, a lot of species of fish are active during the morning, or later in the evening, when the water temperature is cool.

The temperature of the water is another crucial factor to be considered in deciding where to fish. Fish are more active when the water is between 50-80 degrees Fahrenheit. It is crucial to measure into consideration the temp of the waters prior to when you begin fishing. This is done using the use of a thermometer and watching the behaviour and behavior of fish.

It is also essential to take into consideration the accessibility and security of the area. Find locations that are accessible and safe to fish including fish piers or parks that are open to the public. Always follow rules and safety regulations in order to have you have a safe and enjoyable experience fishing.

To conclude, selecting the best location is crucial to a successful freshwater fishing experience. Take into consideration the species of fish you want to catch and the time of day, the water temperature, the accessibility and safety of your spot. If you have the proper information and preparedness will improve your odds of having an enjoyable time on the waters.

Things to take into consideration when choosing the best fishing spots

If you're fishing, finding the ideal location can be the difference between your entire day. No matter if you're an amateur or experienced fisherman spending time to take the time to think about certain aspects will greatly improve your odds of being successful. These are the most important factors to consider while searching for the perfect fishing spot

1. The depth of water - Fish typically live in waters that are deep enough to provide sufficient cover as well as protection against predators. Search for places with an average depth of 6-8 feet. Keep in mind that various species of fish might require different sizes of water.

2. Temperature of Water Fish are cold-blooded animals that means their body temperature is controlled by the temperatures of the water surrounding them. Certain species of fish prefer warmer waters, while other species prefer colder temperatures. Find out about the species of fish you're targeting for their optimal temperature of water.

3. Clear water lets fish discern their prey better which makes it an ideal place to

fish. But, certain species of fish prefer muddy or unclear water, which is why it's essential to identify the kind of water you're seeking.

4. Covers - Fish require protection for protection from predators as well as take advantage of their prey to ambush them. Find areas that have submerged logs, rocks or any other structure which provide the fish with a place to hide.

5. Fish will be attracted to places where they can get foods. Be sure to look for areas with lots of plants or areas those where other fish are eating.

6. Currents are typically encountered in areas that have moderate or even a weak current because it is able to provide oxygen and food to the fish. Certain species, however, prefer locations with more rapid or slower current therefore,

make sure you investigate the specific species that you want to target.

7. Accessibility - Lastly, take into consideration the ease with which you can reach your preferred fishing spot. Are there boat ramps near by? Or can you put your car right at the shoreline? Do you think the location is safe and is it legal to fish in?

If you take these aspects to account, you'll significantly increase your odds to find a winning fishing area. Remember that fishing is about persistence and perseverance So don't let yourself be disappointed even if you do not catch something at first - just keep testing and playing until you locate the place that is most effective for you.

The understanding of water conditions

The understanding of water conditions is vital for anyone who is a beginner and is looking to enhance their chances of landing fish. First, be aware of the various types of water, and the way they impact fish behaviour.

The rivers, lakes and streams each have their own properties that may impact fishing. In the case of a lake that is still like a lake temperatures of the water are likely to remain stable, while the fishing will be scattered. If you are in a stream it is possible for the current to cause it to be more difficult for fish and temperatures may vary much more.

A further important aspect to take into consideration is the water's clarity. Clear waters can make difficult to capture fish because they will be able to discern any risk. However clear water makes fishing easier since they are less likely to get scared.

The depth of water is an additional factor to take into consideration. Diverse species of fish prefer different depths in the water, which is why it's important to identify the kind of fish you're seeking to catch, as well as the depth they prefer.

A second factor to take into consideration is conditions. Water levels can rise when rain falls. to increase, and the increase in flow could create a more difficult task to capture fish. In contrast, cloudy weather could be ideal for fishing because it lowers the amount sunlight in the water which makes it simpler for fish to detect bait.

Alongside these elements the water's conditions could be affected by human activities. Construction, pollution as well as agricultural runoff may be a factor in the water's quality as well as fish behaviour.

# Chapter 16: Types Of Fresh Water Fishing Techniques

## Bait fishing

Bait fishing is among the most popular and successful ways to catch fishing in freshwater. It is the practice of using artificial or live baits for luring fish towards the hook. This is a great method for novices, because it's easy to master and does not require any equipment.

Live bait is by far the most commonly used kind of bait that is used for freshwater fishing. It is comprised of minnows, worms and even insects. The effectiveness of these baits is that they resemble the predators of the fish that you're trying to catch. The most effective method to utilize live bait is hook it either through either the tail or head, dependent on the type of bait you're making use of. This lets it flow naturally through the water and draw fish.

Artificial baits, often referred to as lures, is a well-liked option to fish in freshwater. They come in a wide range of sizes, shapes, and colors. They're made to mimic the movements and look like live bait. A few of the most well-known varieties of lures are spinners, jigs and crankbaits. The lures can be used for catching a range of species of fish, such as trout, bass, and panfish.

If you are choosing a baits for freshwater fishing you must take into consideration the species of fish you intend to catch and the condition of the area you'll fish in. If, for instance, you're fishing in dark water, vibrantly colored lures can perform better than natural baits. Also, if fishing for larger fish for example, pike or bass it is possible to employ live bait instead of lures.

All in all, it is an excellent method to begin freshwater fishing. It's simple to learn and does not require any gear, which makes it suitable for novices. When you're choosing to utilize bait that is live or synthetic be sure to choose the appropriate bait for the type of fish you're fishing for as well as to change the way you present your bait to improve the chances of being successful. If you're able to practice and perseverance, you'll be fishing within less than a minute! time!

Live Bait-Fishing

Live Bait Fishing

Bait fishing using live baits is an incredibly popular method employed by numerous freshwater anglers and it's evident the reason. The use of live bait can prove very effective in catching number of fish. Additionally, is an excellent method to begin your journey into the fishing world. In this chapter that will cover the fundamentals of fishing with live bait, which includes what kinds of baits to choose as well as how to make your bait and the best places you can fish.

Types of Live Bait

The most commonly used kinds of live baits employed in freshwater fishing are minnows and worms as well as the crayfish. Worms are among the most flexible kind of bait that are able to be utilized to catch many different types of fish such as trout, bass as well as panfish. Minnows can be particularly effective at the catch of larger fish including pike and bass. Crayfish make a fantastic choice to catch catfish and other fish living in bottoms.

Rigging Your Bait

There are many methods to set up your live bait based on the type of fish you're hoping to capture. In the case of fishing for panfish, then you could employ a basic hook-and-bobber rig. For bigger fish, like bass, you'll need to make use of a more robust line as well as a slip-sinker rig. Check your local regulations for fishing to make sure your gear is legal.

Where to Fish

If you are using live bait It is important to catch in a suitable location. Find places where you can provide protection for fish like trees that have fallen, weedy beds or outcroppings of sand. Fish often congregate in these places, making these ideal locations to throw your line. Take your time, since it might take time before the fish discover your bait.

The bottom line is that the live bait method is an efficient and simple method to catch many freshwater fish. If you choose the appropriate bait, rigging the line appropriately, and angling at the correct place, you'll improve your odds of getting it right. Be sure to follow the local fishing rules and practices catch-and-release as often as you can. Enjoy your fishing!

Artificial baitfishing

Artificial fishing for baits is an effective method to capture fish that are in fresh water. This is a method using baits and lures to lure fish. is an excellent method to start in the fishing world if you're new. In this section we'll go over all you need to be aware of about fishing with artificial bait and the various types of lures available, how you can choose the best one, and the best way you can use it to capture fish.

Types of Artificial Bait

There are a variety of types of artificial baits, all is designed to replicate different species of prey. The most popular types of artificial baits include:

1. Spinnerbaits: These are lures which have a blade that spins that causes vibration and motion within the water. They are great to catch predatory fish such as pike and bass.

2. Crankbaits are baits that look like small fish or any other prey. They feature a lip which causes them to plunge into the water and attract fish eating at the bottom.

3. Jigs These are baits with a head that is weighted and hook. They're ideal for fishing in areas that have a lot of cover like rock beds, weeds or weeds.

4. Soft Plastics They are lures made out of flexible, soft materials such as silicone or rubber. They're available in a wide range of colors and shapes, and are great to imitate the grubs and worms of prey or any other kind of prey.

Choosing the Right Bait

In selecting a bait made of artificial It is crucial to take into consideration the kind of fish you're attempting to catch and the condition of the waters that you're fishing. In the case of fishing in a lake that is murky then you might want to select a vibrantly colored lure that stands out against the surface. If you're fishing for bass you might want to pick either a crankbait or spinnerbait that replicates the movements of smaller fishing fish.

Using Artificial Bait

If you want to use artificial bait You'll have to put your lure in the water, and slowly reel it back in and mimic your prey's movements the lure is imitating. It is important to alter the speed of your retrieve and how you do it because different species of fish react differently to various types of movements. If you're experiencing no success, you can try shifting to a different style of lure or relocating the location of your bait.

Conclusion

Artificial bait fishing can be a fantastic method to capture freshwater fish. If you have the correct bait, and just a time to practice it is possible to capture a wide variety of species of fish. No matter if you're an amateur or a seasoned angler including artificial bait fishing in your fishing arsenal is an excellent option to boost the amount of fish caught and to have greater fun in the waters.

Fly fishing

Fishing with fly is a well-known method of fishing which involves the use of special fishing equipment that is used to catch fish. The type of fishing used is usually tied to fishing for trout however it could be employed to catch species of fish, too. It requires a little bit of practice and expertise and practice, however it can be an enjoyable and rewarding experience even for those who are new to the sport.

The equipment used for fly fishing comprises the fly rod, reel as well as a line. Fly rods are a lengthy and flexible rod employed to cast the fly line. Fly reels are used to secure the line, as well as to reel in the fish after it has been hooked. The fly line is specific type of fishing line specifically designed to be thrown using your fly rod.

Fishing for fly involves casting a fly line into the water, and applying various techniques to transform the fly into looking like an insect that is natural or any other kind of foods that fish usually consume. It can be accomplished with different kinds of fly flies such as dry flies and wet flies. It can also be done employing different casting methods.

One benefit to fly-fishing is that it permits anglers to go fishing in areas which are hard to access using other fishing equipment. In particular, it is a great method to catch take advantage of small streams and rivers that do not have enough space to cast traditional rods. The fly fishing method can be utilized to take a fish to ponds or lakes with a large amount of vegetation, or other obstructions which make it hard to fish using other kinds of fishing gear.

If you're interested in exploring fly fishing it is crucial to begin with the appropriate equipment and practice your casting skills. It is also advisable to take the class on fly fishing, or enlisting a guide to assist you in getting to where you want to be. By a little training and perseverance it is possible to be a proficient fly-fisherman and experience the excitement of fishing in the air.

## Wet fly fishing

The fishing of the wet is an old technique used throughout the ages to capture fish. It's an excellent choice for people beginning to fishing in the fresh water, since it's fairly easy to master and is extremely efficient. In this chapter we'll discuss the fundamentals of wet-fly fishing. We will also discuss its purpose, the best way you can do it, as well as the types of fish are available by using this method.

## What is Wet Fly Fishing?

Wet fly fishing is a type of fishing that requires the angler to will cast a fly made to sink beneath the water's surface. The majority of the time, the fly is comprised of fur, feathers as well as other substances to resemble baitfish, insects, and other animals that fish love to consume. When the fly is dropped in the waters, it sinks into the water to where fish feed The angler then uses an array of quick and jerky movements that allow the fly to move as the real baitfish or an insect.

How to Do Wet Fly Fishing?

For you to begin wet fly fishing You will require some basic equipment like the fly rod reel, line, along with a few wet fiddlers. Additionally, you will need to master the fundamental casting methods employed in fly fishing that involve whipping motion that allows you to cast the line onto the waters.

Once you're prepared to go fishing, you'll have to select the appropriate type of wet fly that is appropriate for the environment you're fishing in. There are many types of wet flies that are made to mimic different types of bugs or baitfish Some work better in particular kind of waters or during different seasons of the year.

What kind of fish can be caught with wet Fly Fishing?

Wet fly fishing is utilized to catch a vast assortment of freshwater species, like bass, trout panfish, and many others. The trick is to pick the appropriate type of wet fly to catch the species you are targeting and apply the correct methods to make it move in a manner to entice fishing fish to take it.

Wet fly fishing is an excellent method for those who are seeking to start their journey into freshwater fishing. If you are able to practice it with the proper tools and methods and you'll be fishing for fish within very little time!

Dry fly fly fishing is among the most thrilling and difficult kinds of fishing in freshwater. It is the use of a light artificial fly, which floats over the surface of the water in order to resemble insects, and attract fish. This type of fishing demands the ability and perseverance, however it's incredibly satisfying when it is done right.

In order to begin with dry fly-fishing, you'll require the fly rod, reel and a line. Additionally, you'll require a range of dry flies that come in a variety of dimensions and colors that match the aquatic insects. In selecting the flies you'll need, it is important to think about the species of fish you're after as well as the time of the year.

After you've bought your equipment It's time to locate a place to take a fish. You should look for calm, slow-moving and clear water that is full of insects. The best rule of thumb is to cast your flies upwards and let it move effortlessly with the current. If you notice an animal rise up towards the fly, you should wait for a few seconds before putting the hook. It will allow your fish time to swallow the entire fly into the mouth of its.

Dry fly fishing is difficult, however it's extremely satisfying. The excitement of watching the fish swim towards your fly only to catch it is unparalleled. You must remember it's a Catch-and-Release game. Make sure you handle the fish in a gentle manner and let it go back in the water as fast as you can.

Dry fly fishing can be described as an enjoyable and demanding type of freshwater fishing that needs skill, patience as well as the appropriate equipment. After a few hours of training and practice, you'll learn to imitate insect movements and catch fish with the same skill as a professional. Be gentle to the fish, and then release the fish quickly once you have caught the fish. Enjoy fishing!

Spinning

Spinning is a very popular method employed by a lot of beginner fisherman to catch freshwater fish. It's an excellent opportunity to get a grasp of the basics of fishing. It can be utilized in all sorts of various settings, from lakes and ponds, to streams and rivers.

For you to begin spinning, you'll require an appropriate spinning rod as well as a reel. They are specially designed specifically for spinning and will aid you in casting your line more effectively and also with greater precision. When choosing your rod and reel, ensure that you select the appropriate size to the kind of fish you're targeting.

In the case of bait, spinning may be employed with live or artificial baits. Common choices include worms baits, minnows and other lures. Be sure to choose the correct type of bait for the species you're aiming for and the environment that you'll be fishing.

For casting your line, use both hands, and then use the dominant hand to hold the reel. The other hand should keep the line close to the rod's highest point. Reverse the rod over your shoulder, and then swiftly move it forward, dislodging the line in doing this. The bait or lure should be able to hit the water with splash. Try casting it on a flat surface before testing it on the surface.

When your line has been placed in the water, it's time to reel it into. Turn the handle slowly on the reel. Use your rod in order to provide your lure or bait some motion. This helps lure fish to you and increase their likelihood to take the bait. Be aware of your line, and prepare to put the hook in place in the event that you feel a pull or feel the line begin moving.

## Chapter 17: Spin Casting

Spin casting is an extremely popular method for fishing that is suitable for novices and more experienced anglers. This is an incredibly versatile method that is suitable for many freshwater ecosystems and can be employed to catch a broad variety of species of fish.

The fundamental idea of spin casting is to throw an object or lure into the water by using the spinning reel and rod. The reel sits above the rod, and it is made to spin when the line is pulled out. The spinning motion helps propel the lure in the water, which makes it easier to cast further and more accurately.

One of the major benefits of spinning casting is that it's very easy to master and learn to master. After a little practice beginning anglers can master casting and reeling in fish with the technique. It's also an cost-effective and easily accessible method to fish, since spinning casting equipment is readily accessible at a lot of fishing retail shops.

For the first time to begin spinning casting, you'll require the basics of equipment. There is an angling rod and spinning reel and a fishing spool line, as well as a range of baits and lures. It is essential to select the appropriate gear that is appropriate for the kind of fish that you intend to target and the location you'll fish in.

If you are casting using the spin casting reel it's important to make the motion in a fluid, smooth manner. Begin with the rod's end pointed towards the water. Then, rapidly snap it backwards by whipping it. The rod will move forward you can release it with the push of a release button of the reel. Find a place on the surface where it is possible that fish are in the area, then remove the bait or lure by reeling it back into.

All in all, it's an excellent method for novices to master and learn. If you can master it with a little practicing and using the correct equipment, you'll rapidly become an experienced angler, and begin catching many freshwater species of fish.

Spinning

Spinning is an extremely popular method of fishing that utilizes the spinning reel along with rods to cast fishing lure or bait. Spinning is an effective method which can be utilized in diverse freshwater fishing conditions like lakes, rivers and ponds. Spinning is a good option for novices as it's very easy to learn and the equipment is inexpensive and readily available.

For spinning to begin the reel, you'll require spinning reels as well as a spinning rod fishing line and fishing lure, or bait. Spinning reels are built to be mounted onto the rod and are very easy to control.

The rod that spins is flexible, and comes with guides to help the line glide effortlessly. The fishing line is crucial and should be sturdy enough to support any weight that the species you're trying to catch. Bait or lure is what draws the fishing fish to bite.

When you are deciding on an appropriate bait or lure it is important to think about the species of fish that you're aiming for and the specific conditions under which you'll be fishing. If, for instance, you're fishing in the murky waters, you might choose a vibrantly colored lure that will help fish better see the lure. If you're fishing for bass, then you might want to consider using spinnerbaits. They are an imitation of the movement of a fish that has fled.

To cast a reel spinning to cast, you must hold the rod in both hands, keeping your elbows in close proximity the body. Keep the rod in your index finger and using a flick of your wrist, let go of the line, pointing your rod towards the direction you'd like to cast it. While the lure moves through the water you'll be able to feel for strikes or tugs on the line. If you sense that there is a fish in the line, pull it in gradually and slowly with tension maintained in the line.

In the end the spinning technique is a great method of fishing for novices. It's simple to learn cost-effective, versatile, and affordable. With just a little time and effort and practice, you'll be an expert spinner, and also get a lot of fish on the freshwater you go on.

The Art of Casting

Casting basics

The basics of casting are vital to be successful in freshwater fishing. Casting is casting your lure or bait in the water to draw fishing. It's important to know the basics of the casting process prior to heading into the water.

First thing you should consider while casting is the kind of equipment you'll use. There are two kinds of gear that are used for freshwater fishing, casting and spinning. The spinning gear is typically easier to learn for novices because it takes less skill and training. Baitcasting equipment however is more complex and takes a lot of training to be mastered.

When you've picked the correct equipment The next thing to do is to master the correct casting method. The most fundamental casting method is an overhead casting. To cast this way make sure you hold the rod using your hands, then bring the rod back to your shoulders. Next, move the rod towards you and let loose your line at the proper time so that the lure or bait go into the water.

A different technique that you should master is to master the side-arm cast. This is a great technique to use for casting through low hanging branches or any another obstruction. For this casting use the rod using one hand, and then bring it towards the side, close to the surface of water. Next, you should bring the rod inward and let go of the line, allowing the lure or bait to fly off into the pool of water.

Also, it is important to know how to rolling cast. This method is helpful for casting within tight areas or when wind is coming in the direction of your face. To cast a roll take the rod back onto your shoulder, then move it forward in a swift movement, halting your rod abruptly towards the point where you have completed the cast. The line will begin to move out in front of you and allow the lure or bait to drop into the lake.

## Casting types

Casting is a crucial ability for freshwater fishing. This is the act of casting a fishing line or bait into the ocean to capture fish. There are many different kinds of casting methods, each of which serves an individual purpose. Below are the most commonly used varieties of casting techniques that are employed in freshwater fishing

### 1. Overhead Cast

The overhead casting technique is the most fundamental and popular casting technique used in freshwater fishing. This is an easy method that requires you to swing the rod of fishing over your head before casting it forward. This casting technique is suitable for medium to short distances. It is great for the capture of small or medium-sized fish.

### 2. Sidearm Cast

Sidearm casting is similar to overhead casting, however, the rod is held horizontally, and in a parallel position with the floor. It is appropriate to catch fish in small areas or casting beneath the branches that are low or over obstacles.

3. Roll Cast

Roll casting is a method used to fishing in places where there is a small amount of room to move the rod. It is a method of rolling the line across the water's surface, and shifting the rod inwards and casting it. It is a great method to capture fish in tiny streams and creeks.

4. Spey Cast

Spey casting is a casting method that can be done with two hands that is used to fish in bigger body of water, like lakes or rivers. The technique involves using a longer rod with a long line to cast longer with little effort. This method is perfect to catch large fish like steelhead or salmon.

5. Pitch Cast

It is a method that is used to fish in small space or for casting beneath obstructions. It is accomplished by flipping the lure underhand before letting it fall gently on the water. This method is perfect to catch fish that are hiding beneath hanging branches or in other areas.

To conclude, understanding the diverse casting techniques is the most important thing for any freshwater angler. By practicing and being patient will help you enhance your casting abilities and improve your odds of landing more fish. If you're a novice or seasoned angler understanding the various techniques for casting will make fishing trip much more enjoyable and rewarding.

Enhancing your casting skills

Casting is among the essential skills that you should be able to master in order to become successful in the field of freshwater fishing. Casting is the art of putting your bait and fishing line into the water with a method which attracts fish and aid in catching the fish. Here are some suggestions that will help you develop your casting ability.

1. Practice or practice, practise, practice

The more time you spend practicing casting, the better become in this area. Choose a peaceful spot in which you can work without distracting factors, like parks or in a backyard. Begin by casting for short distances, and then gradually increasing the distance of your casting when you feel more confident.

2. Utilize the appropriate equipment

Be sure to have the correct equipment to meet your casting requirements. If your rod is weighty or light could cause casting to be difficult. An overly length can cause it to be difficult to cast precisely. Select a rod that has an appropriate length and weight. will work for the kind of fishing that you want to pursue.

3. Make sure you are using the correct technique

There are a variety of casting techniques and every is suitable for different styles of fishing and different conditions. Know the basics of casting including overhead casting, the sidearm cast as well as roll cast. You should learn them until you are able to perform them effortlessly. Diverse types of baits and lures need different casting methods So be sure to modify your approach depending on the bait you're applying to.

4. Be aware of the direction of wind

Wind could have an effect on the casting precision of your. If you are experiencing wind at your back then you'll need adapt your method to adjust. Cast at an angle relative to winds, or try an extra heavy lure or bait to aid in cutting your line through the breeze.

5. Watch your line

Pay attention to your line while casting your line, and make sure you remain in an even line as it travels across the air. If the line begins to curve, alter your method to correct the curve. Straight lines will aid you cast more precisely.

Enhancing your casting ability is a process that takes time and effort It's well worth it. By following these guidelines and techniques, you'll be in the process of becoming a proficient freshwater fisherman.

Fresh Water Fishing Safety

## Be aware of safety precautions

Being aware of safety measures is essential to every outdoor pursuit, but especially with regard to freshwater fishing. No matter if you're a beginner or an experienced fisherman, it's important that you consider safety as the primary factor to guarantee an enjoyable and successful fishing experience.

One of the most important things you need to think about when making plans for your trip to fish is conditions. Make sure to check the forecast before you go out. Also, beware of fishing in extreme conditions like severe winds or storms. Be sure to put on a suitable outfit and an appropriate life jacket while fishing from a vessel.

Another important security measure is to carry an emergency kit. Unexpected accidents can occur with a properly-stocked kit will help manage minor injuries, and also prevent injuries from getting more serious. The most important items you should include in your first-aid kit include adhesive bandages antiseptic gauze, wipes also medical tape.

Also, it is important to keep an eye on your surroundings when fishing. Be aware of the surroundings around you, and be aware of all potential hazards like the cliffs, steep drop, or underwater obstructions. Also, you should be aware of wildlife could be in your path including bears, snakes or alligators.

If you are fishing with someone else be sure to communicate clearly and set the rules and guidelines to ensure everybody's security. This means setting up a defined fishing zone and agreeing the exact distance that each angler must be from the other when they cast.

## Chapter 18: Emergency Preparedness

One of the main factors to be aware of when you go on a fishing expedition is the need to be prepared for emergencies. However experienced you are or how carefully you plan your trip, mishaps or unexpected incidents can occur. It is important to prepare for every situation that might happen while on the water.

In the first place, be sure that you've got a first aid kit at the ready. It should have items like bandages antiseptic ointment and pain relief and all the medications needed. Also, ensure that you include plenty of water as well as food in the event that you are lost or stuck.

A crucial factor in emergency preparedness is the ability to stay in touch with other people in the world. Cell phones or a two-way radio could be life-saving in the event of a crisis. Always ensure you've got an energized phone or radio always Consider bringing an extra charger and portable batteries in case of.

It's important to stay well-informed about the local climate and the forecast prior to leaving. If you're concerned about stormy weather, think about rescheduling your fishing excursion. If you're already in the water, and a weather system is forming, make sure you get towards shore as soon as you can.

Make sure that someone has your itinerary. Before leaving, let someone in your family or a close friend know the location you'll be fishing, and the time you'll be to be back. If you fail to return by the scheduled time then they'll be aware to call the authorities.

Preparedness for emergencies may not appear to be the most thrilling aspect of fishing, however it's an essential aspect to being safe in the waters. If you take time to take the time to be prepared for every scenario, you'll be able take advantage of your fishing experience without worry.

Fishing etiquette

The manner of fishing is an essential element of a fishing excursion. It is crucial to adhere to some guidelines and regulations so that the trip is enjoyable for all those involved. In this section we'll go over what is acceptable and not acceptable the fishing industry.

In the first place, you must be considerate of the other fishermen who are on the waters. If you are fishing close to other fishermen, try not to occupy the area and casting in the direction of others. Also, try not to make too much noises or disrupting the tranquility of the surroundings. Keep in mind that everyone is here for peace and enjoyment in the outdoors.

Also, make sure you adhere to the rules and regulations that govern the area where fishing is allowed. These regulations exist in order to protect fish and the ecosystem, as well as to assure that everyone is given the same chance to catch a fish. It is crucial to be familiar with guidelines before you start fishing.

Always be sure to practice catch and release. It means that you have to release all fish is caught back in lake, preferably in the case of fish that are tiny or if you've already caught the limit. This is a way to protect the population of fish and guarantees that future generations will be able to enjoy fishing, too.

Fourthly, ensure that your surroundings are neat and tidy. Be sure to eliminate your garbage correctly and leave your area clean and tidy as you left it. This will help preserve the beauty of nature in the place and guarantees that it is a relaxing area to fish.

Always be polite and helpful to fellow fishing enthusiasts. Be willing to assist if you feel you need assistance, and offer ideas and techniques if you are curious. Remember that fishing is a communal activity and everybody is there to have fun together.

The bottom line is that good fishing manners is a crucial element of a fishing excursion. When you are able to practice proper etiquette and etiquette, you will be able to ensure everyone enjoys a pleasant and enjoyable fishing trip. Be respectful adhere to the rules, practise catch and release Keep your fishing area spotless and friendly to other fishermen. Have fun fishing!

Catching and Handling Fresh Water Fish

How do you hook and capture the fish

One of the best things about freshwater fishing is the excitement of hooking up and fishing. If you're just starting out or an expert angler there are several important techniques and tips that will improve your odds of getting the job done.

In the first place, it's essential to pick the appropriate bait or lure to match the species of fish you're aiming for. There are different species of fish that have distinct preferences regarding eating, and you'll have to conduct some studies or talk to local experts which ones work best for the area you live in. The most popular choices are minnows, worms, synthetic lures, as well as Flies.

When you've picked your lure after which you've chosen your bait, it's time to make your cast. It can be a challenge for those who are new to fishing, and it's essential to master your method before going into the waters. Start by holding the rod using both hands while pull the line in front of your back. After that, make an arcing motion to push the line in a forward direction and release it at the proper moment so that the lure or bait fall into the waters.

When your bait is sinking and sinks, keep an watch on the line and prepare to take action whenever you feel a tug or feel a sudden shift. In the event that you receive a strike you want to make sure that you place the hook swiftly and securely by pulling back your rod. The hook will be firmly encased into the fish's mouth which makes it much easier to reel it in.

After you've caught a fish, the excitement starts! Make use of your reel to gently and gradually take the fish into the water making sure not to let it escape. Based on the size and power of your fish, it could be anywhere from a couple of seconds to a few hours. If you are able to get your fish near enough to the boat or shoreline using a net or your hands to release the hook before releasing the fish into the lake.

In the end, the most important thing for catching and hooking fish is to remain attentive, patient and determined. If you're able to practice it and have appropriate tools, you'll reel into big fish within very little time!

Best practices for handling fish

For a novice fisherman it's important to master the most effective methods for handling fish, to ensure their continued survival as well as the long-term sustainability of our waterways. Below are some suggestions to keep in mind:

1. Be sure to clean your hands prior to taking a bite of fish. This will help protect the slime layer that is crucial to boost their immunity and defense against parasites.

2. Make use of barbless hooks, or simply cut the barbs off of the hooks. This will make it much easier to pull the hook out and less damaging to the mouth of the fish.

3. If you are planning to let the fish go, take it easy and quickly. Do not keep them from the water too time, and also help them to support their weight using both hands. If it is possible, let them go when they're still submerged.

4. If you are required to take care of a fish, it is best to be careful when handling a fish. Make use of a rubberized net in order in order to protect the fins or scales of their fish, as well as avoid pressing their fins too tight.

5. If you are planning keeping the fish in your tank, eliminate them swiftly and safely. An abrasive strike to the head, or a

cut on the gills is both successful ways to do so.

6. Make sure to clean your equipment following each use in order to stop the transmission of parasites or diseases in waters.

7. Be aware of limits on catch as well as size limitations within your region. These rules are put in place in order to safeguard the long-term sustainability of our fishing industry.

If you follow these guidelines by following these best practices, you will help ensure the protection of the fish as well as the habitat for future generations of anglers. Keep in mind that the most crucial part of fishing isn't simply catching fish however, it is also a way of caring for the environment that surrounds us.

Cleansing and cleaning the fish and preparation is an integral element of fishing. Prior to enjoying the delicious meal of fish it is essential to wash and cook your catch. The process isn't easy to those who are new, however with just a couple of steps, you'll be able to have a flawlessly ready fish in a short time.

The first step is to collect your cleaning tools. It's best to have a sharp, fillet knife, a cutting table as well as a bucket of pure water. It's also recommended to put on gloves in order to shield your hands from sharp bone.

After you've caught your catch It's time to wash it. First, wash the fish in the bucket with clear water. After that, you can use a fillet knife and make cuts just below the gills, and then through into the belly of the fish. Make sure not to cut the fish too deeply otherwise you risk puncturing the internal organs.

Then, you can use your fillet knife for removing the entrails as well as any other organs inside. It is also possible to cut off the tail and head in the event that you would prefer. Rinse the fish once more in clean water in order to wash off any remaining dirt or blood.

Then it's time for filleting the fish. Set the fish down on the cutting board, and create a cut right below the head and downwards towards the backbone. After that, you can use the filet knife through the backbone. Keep the blade firmly against the bone. Repeat the process on the other side of the fish.

When you've finished filletings then you'll need to take out any bones that remain using the tweezers, or even a fishing bone plier. Rinse the fish fillets under the fresh water for a second time before you're ready to cook.

There are a variety of methods of cooking fresh fish from cooking to baking, to grilling and finally fry. Try different recipes to determine which one is best for your needs. Keep in mind that the cleaner fish you can get, the more delicious it is.

With these instructions, you will be able to wash and prepare fresh seafood with ease. Do not be afraid of the method - with some practicing, you'll be an pro within the shortest time. Have fun fishing!

Fresh Water Fishing Tips and Tricks

For beginners, here are some tips.

If you're just beginning to learn on the waters of freshwater fishing this article is perfect ideal for those who are new to fresh water fishing. Fishing is a thrilling and enjoyable experience, however it's also frustrating in the event that you don't understand the basics of what you're doing. Here are a few tips to get you going:

## 1. Find the best equipment

Before you begin fishing, make sure you be equipped with the proper equipment. You'll need the fishing rod reel and line, as well as hooks as well as bait. They can be bought in a local sporting goods shop or even online. You should ensure that you purchase the correct size and kind of equipment for the kind of fish you wish to capture.

## 2. Get the fundamentals

It is essential to master the fundamentals of fishing prior to you get started. Learn the art of knotting and cast a line and reel in the catch. Online tutorials are available or find a person who has experience fishing to demonstrate.

## 3. Select the correct place

The right place to fish is vital to catch the fish. Research the area that you wish to fish and determine what kind of fish live in the waters. Also, you can ask residents or park rangers information on fishing spots.

## 4. Be patient

Fishing requires patience. There is a chance that you will not be able to catch fish immediately Therefore, it's essential to keep striving. There may be a need to modify your bait, or go into a new location in order in order to improve your odds of landing a fish.

## 5. Be respectful of the earth

Respect the natural environment while fishing. You must comply with the regulations and rules of the region you're fishing. It is also important to tidy up after yourself and do not leave any garbage left behind.

## 6. Training in Catch and Release

If you don't plan on eating the fish that you capture, you must learn to capture and release. It means that you must let the fish go back to the sea in a safe manner. This will help preserve the fish population, and also ensures that the next generation can continue to also enjoy fishing.

The tips above can assist you in getting started on the right foot with fresh water fishing. Be sure to enjoy yourself and have fun. Fishing is an excellent opportunity to relax and reconnect with the natural world.

## Chapter 19: Techniques For Advanced Use

When you've learned the fundamentals of freshwater fishing, it is possible to learn more advanced methods that will help you get bigger and more difficult fish. Here are some suggestions and tips to boost your fishing up a notch.

1. Utilize live baits: While artificial lures work but live bait is much more effective at the attraction of fish. You can try using minnows, worms or crayfish as baits to entice your target.

2. Test various depths: Fish may be seen at different depths based on time of day and weather conditions. Test various depths by altering your bait, or employing a weighted line to make your bait go deeper.

3. Make use of a fishfinder: Fish finders are gadget that makes use of sonar technology to identify fish that are in the waters. It helps you find groups of fish and measure their depth. This makes it much easier to locate the fish.

4. Sight fishing is a method of fishing that is based on looking for fish on the water and casting your lure directly into their

direction. It takes patience and attentive eye, however it is very satisfying.

5. Fly fishing is an advanced method that requires the use of a special rod and reel to throw light-weight fly lines into the lake. This requires practice but is a fun method of catching fish.

6. Night fishing: Fish tend to be more active during the night which is why fishing in the dark could be an effective method to capture these fish. Utilize a lamp to lure fishermen to the bait Be sure to carry a flashlight to ensure security.

7. Trolling involves the dragging of a bait or lure behind a boat that is moving. It is effective in taking larger fish but will require a boat as well as special equipment.

The advanced techniques for fishing could take your freshwater fishing to a new stage. Remember, practicing and perseverance are essential for becoming an effective angler. Enjoy fishing!

Tips and hacks for fishing

Fishing is a thrilling outdoors activity that is loved by any age. It's an excellent opportunity to get in touch with the natural world, spend some time with your loved ones, spend quality time with your family and friends and also catch some tasty seafood for dinner. It can also be a challenge for novices who don't have the appropriate tools or know-how. This is why we've put together the best fishing tips and techniques that can aid you in becoming a successful angler in a short time.

1. Make sure you are using the correct method of bait

Fish will be attracted by different kinds of baits, based on species and time of the year. Fish that prefer live bait while other are drawn to lures and artificial bait. Research the kind of fish you'd like to capture, and then use the right bait. Also, you can test different kinds of bait to find out which ones work best.

2. Watch out for the conditions

The weather's influence on the behaviour of fish. When it is sunny the fish will stay within deeper waters to escape the heat. On daytime clouds, they can relocate to more shallow waters for food. Additionally, wind may affect flow of the water and make difficult to capture fish. Be sure to look up the weather forecast prior to you go out, and then adjust your strategy for fishing accordingly.

3. Be patient

The sport of fishing requires lots of patience. There is a chance that you will have to wait for several hours before catching any fish, but never abandon the pursuit. Place your fishing line in the water, and then wait for the fish to strike. If you're having no luck at one location Try moving to a new area.

## 4. Use polarized sunglasses

Polarized sunglasses help identify fish by decreasing glare and improving visibility. It is particularly helpful for fishing in water that is shallow or when you are in bright light.

## 5. Be sure to cast properly

An accurate cast is vital to a success in fishing. Cast in a clean location prior to going into the ocean. Make sure to cast in a fluid, smooth movement and try to find an area where you believe you might find a fish.

## 6. Keep your gear organized

An unorganized tackle box could take up a lot of time and lead to irritation. Make sure your equipment is neat and easy to access in order to swiftly swap off lures and bait.

If you follow these tips and tips If you follow these fishing hacks and tricks, you'll be in the process of being a professional angler. Be sure to follow all the regulations of fishing, and to do your best to practice catch and release whenever it is possible to conserve the natural resources we have. Enjoy fishing!

Fresh Water Fishing and the Environment

Knowing the ecology

The understanding of the ecosystem is an essential aspect of freshwater fishing. The ecosystem is an intricate system made up of living and non-living elements who work together to produce an environment that is balanced. For a beginner it is vital to comprehend how the ecosystem functions in order to maximize your chances of landing fish, and also to be sure you're doing no harm to the ecosystem.

The ecology of a freshwater reservoir comprises a variety of elements, such as the water, the submerged of the substrata, vegetation animal, microorganisms, and plants. Each component play a crucial role in the overall wellbeing that the entire ecosystem. In particular, plants create oxygen, and provide shelter as well as food for the fish and aquatic animals. Microorganisms breakdown dead animal and plant matter and provide nutrients to different organisms within the ecosystem.

## Chapter 20: Understanding Striped Bass Behavior And Characteristics

Striped bass is among the most sought-after game fish found in the Atlantic Ocean and coastal rivers. Understanding their behaviors and features is crucial to catch the fish consistently. In this section we'll explore the life-cycle and biology of striped bass and also their eating habits, as well as their preferred locations.

Biology and Life Cycle

Striped bass (Morone saxatilis) is a native of The Atlantic coastline that runs through North America, from the St. Lawrence River to the Gulf of Mexico. It is a migratory species that spends the summer in the northern waters, and winters in south. Striped bass are spawned in streams and rivers that are freshwater throughout springtime and summer, when adults move towards the upper reaches of streams to spawn that have a suitable gravel or rocky substrate.

Striped bass is a part of the family Moronidae comprising several different species of game fish including white perch as well as hybrid the striped bass. They are able to live for up to 30 years old, however the majority of striped bass caught anglers are aged between 3 to 10 years old. Adult striped bass can get as long as 4 feet and weigh up to 50 pounds. But the majority fishing caught by recreational anglers have a length of 20-30 inches and weigh between 5 and 15 pounds.

Feeding Habits

Striped bass can be considered opportunistic feeders that means they can eat nearly anything they catch. The species they prefer to eat is dependent on the location they are in and time of the year. In estuaries and rivers the striped bass take small fish, including herring white perch, shad and Eels. When they are in their ocean habitat, they devour larger fish, such as menhaden, squid as well as other baitfish.

In the summer, the striped bass are active throughout all daylight hours. When the autumn arrives the fish begin feeding much more frequently in anticipation of their move to the south. In the winter months, stripe bass are less active and eat less often.

Preferred Habitats

Striped bass are located in many habitats, ranging from deep oceans to the shallows of streams and rivers. They are attracted to temperatures of 55 to 68°F and require high-quality water to live. Water that is oxygen rich and clean is crucial for young striped bass, to stay alive and develop.

Adult striped bass are present in various habitats such as rocky shorelines, beaches with sand, jetties and close to submerged structures like wrecks and reefs. The species also assemble at areas where prey species are plentiful, like areas where rivers run into the ocean, or in areas in areas where baitfish meet.

Knowing the behavior of striped bass and its specific characteristics is an important aspect of fishing success. If you know which areas and times to hunt for stripe bass and the species they might be eating fishing, anglers increase the chances of landing these difficult to catch game fish. In the next sections, we'll look at the tackle and gear available as well as baits and lures as well as fishing methods that work best when catching striped bass various locations and under different circumstances.

## Chapter 21: Gear And Tackle Choosing The Right Fishing Equipment

In the case of catching stripe bass, using the appropriate gear and equipment is vital. This will not only improve your chances of getting the largest fish however, it can also enhance the enjoyment in general. In this section we'll look at the diverse kinds of tackle and gear which are ideal for fishing Striped Bass and how you can choose the most suitable equipment to meet your needs.

Rods and Reels

Selecting the correct reel and rod can significantly impact your chances of successfully catching striped bass. There are numerous kinds of reels and rods to choose from which is why it's crucial to determine what you're searching for prior to purchasing.

If you want to catch stripe bass, using a moderate to heavy-action reel is recommended since the fish can give a tough fight. With regards to reels, a reel that spins is an option that is popular because it's simple to use and is versatile. But, there are anglers who choose baitcasting reels because of their control and accuracy.

A crucial aspect to consider is that the reel must be set up to match the rod in a proper way. Incorrectly matched gear could make fishing uncomfortable and difficult, and can cause additional stress on the equipment and the fish.

Line

The selection of the best line is a crucial aspect to consider. It's crucial to pick one that's sturdy and long-lasting enough to withstand the power and fighting of stripe bass. Braided line is an extremely popular option due to its strength and can take on the power of a huge species of fish. Monofilament lines are also an excellent choice, especially to those who appreciate the flexibility and forgiving character of mono.

In selecting a line it's important to also consider the testing of the line's pounds. The pound test is the weight the line will hold before breaking. If you are looking for striped bass, a 20-30lb test line is suggested.

Terminal Tackle

Terminal tackle refers to apparatus that attaches to the line at the bottom of the line used for fishing. That includes hooks, sinkers and swivels as well as leaders. Selecting the correct terminal tackle is essential since it directly impacts the chances of you catching stripe bass.

When choosing hooks you must select the right size to match the bait's size to be used. Sizes of either 1/0 or 2/0 simple shank hook can be the ideal choice for all circumstances. If you are using live bait circular hooks are usually chosen because they catch the fish at the part of the mouth that is in the corner which makes it simpler hook removal.

Size of sinker is contingent on the water's depth and the power of the flow. The general rule is to select the tiniest sinker to achieve the depth you want to reach. The use of a larger weight may make the bait appear strange and can deter fishing fish from biting.

The swivels can be used to avoid the twist of lines and create knots. When choosing swivels it is important to select an appropriate size for your length of the line as well as the dimension of the fish.

Leader material is an additional piece of line connected between the mainline and the hook. Leader material is crucial to fish for the striped bass since it is able to be eaten by the sharp teeth of the fish. The fluorocarbon leader material is the most popular option since it is virtually undetectable in waters and is characterized by its high scratch resistance.

Bait and Lures

In the end, lures and bait are a vital element of fishing for stripe bass. Live baits such as Eels, clams, or bunker are also popular as they are extremely effective in the capture of stripe bass.

## Chapter 22: Selecting The Best Options For Striped Bass

Selecting the Best Options for Striped Bass

The selection of lures and baits can be an overwhelming challenge for anglers of all levels, but it is particularly difficult when you are targeting an animal like the stripe bass. There's a myriad of lures and bait options which can be employed to catch striped bass the Atlantic Ocean and coastal rivers. In this article you'll learn the most effective bait and lure choices for striped bass, as well as the best ways to utilize them.

Bait Selection:

If you are looking to select baits for striped bass you can choose from a range of options, such as dead bait, live bait, or cut bait. Live bait is usually the most efficient bait as it moves and looks alive for the fish. A few popular live baits are sandworms and eels and mackerel. Important to keep in mind that the size of the bait you choose to use is to be proportional to what size stripe bass that you intend to catch. In general, a baitfish which measures about 1/3 of the size of the prey fish will be a good standard.

Cut bait or dead bait choices can work, however they should be utilized properly to draw stripe bass. The most popular dead baits are squid, clams and mackerel. When you use dead baits is crucial to recognize that the smell of the bait is going to draw the attention of the striped bass. For the best scent from the bait, make sure that you are using fresh bait and the hook is rigged properly using the head, or flesh strip.

Lure Selection:

They are a popular choice for pursuing striped bass since they're versatile and may be utilized to cover vast amount of water fast. If you are looking for a suitable lure to target the striped bass, there's a myriad of varieties to look at, such as plugs, jigs, and soft plastic lures. Below are some of the top lures to catch striped bass:

1. Jigs: Jigs can be one of the most efficient baits to catch the striped bass. They're available in a vast variety of sizes and weights that make them suitable to different depths and flows. Jigs that are topped with soft plastic bait like an elongated tail, could replicate the movement that live bait makes.

2. Plugs: Plugs make excellent lures for stripe bass as they are able to mimic the appearance of baitfish. They are available in a range of sizes and shapes. are able to mimic various swimming movements depending on the shape.

3. Soft plastic baits: Soft baits, such as swimbaits or Grubs, are effective lures to eat stripe bass. They provide a real-feel as well as a swim action, making the perfect choice for to use when stripe bass feed on smaller baitfish.

It's crucial to keep in mind that different lures are effective in various conditions. For instance, a jig might be more effective in turbulent waters, whereas an e-lure might be best suitable for waters with less roughness. Test different lures, and then adjust your method according to the environment.

## Chapter 23: Fundamental Skills For Successful Fishing

If you are a striped bass angler knowing and mastering the fundamental knots and rigs are crucial capabilities to possess for success fishing. A properly knotted rig and knot will make all the impact on the number of fish you catch as well as the efficiency with which you catch the fish. In this section we'll provide a brief overview of the best knots and rigs to catch the striped bass.

Knots for Striped Bass Fishing:

These knots are the most important knots to learn in order to be a success in striped bass fishing.

1. Palomar Knot:

It is one of the strongest and easiest to tie knots that is suitable for anglers of all level. It's perfect for attaching braided line or fluorocarbon hooks to lures and swings.

For tying the Palomar knot take these instructions:

Double the length of the line. Then run it through the eye of the hook to lure, or turn.

Create a loose and open overhand knot. Make sure the knot is big enough to allow the hook to go through.

Take the doubled ends of the line and pass it around the loop you've made. Following this, tie a loose knot overhand.

Keep your hook, lure, or the swivel with one hand, and the line that is doubled in the opposite hand. Then pull each end of the line until you make the knot tighter.

2. Improved Clinch Knot:

The knot makes a fantastic solution for securing lures or hooks onto monofilament or fluorocarbon lines. This knot has been improved to be an extremely durable knot which can stand up to the pressure of a large fish. When you tie your Improved Clinch Knot, follow these instructions:

Thread the line into to the eyes of hook to lure or swivel.

Grab the hook or lure with one hand, and then take the line's end using the other hand.

Make 5-7 turns in the direction of the standing line, ending at the tag.

Push the tag's end through the loop created at the time you held the hook and line.

Moisten the knot by rubbing it with saliva or water in your mouth. Then tighten the knot by a soft tug.

3. Double Dropper Loop:

This loop is ideal to set up an introductory system to lure bass. The loop has two hooks which permit anglers to catch multiple lures or baits. For tying to the Double Dropper Loop, follow these steps:

Begin by making an overhand knot loosely in the line approximately 8 to 10 inches over the end to the line.

Create a tiny loop. Pass the ends of the line into the knot you tied earlier. Make a larger loop, then repeat the loop.

Start pulling the end of the line until you tie the knot. It is recommended to have two loops, or droppers of similar size that you can tie your lures.

Rigs for Striped Bass Fishing:

Being aware of and understanding what to do when it comes time to tie fishing rods in landing striped bass. Below are some efficient and simple-to-tie fishing rigs that are suitable to catch stripe bass.

1. Fish Finder Rig:

The rig for fishing fish is the most versatile and efficient device for fishing in the surf to catch stripe bass. It's made to secure the bait on its tack and allow it to naturally move with the flow of the. In order to tie the fishfinder rig, you'll require these items:

Fishing line

Weight of the fish

Barrel swivel

Monofilament or fluorocarbon leader

## Chapter 24: Understanding Their Habits And Habitats

The understanding of the habitat and behaviour of striped bass are crucial for increasing the chances of being successful in catching these fish. Striped bass are anadromous meaning they reproduce in freshwater but spend most of their time in saltwater. Striped bass are found in the coasts across to the Gulf of St. Lawrence from Canada all the way to in the Gulf of Mexico, but they're the most common in the region of Maine from Maine to North Carolina.

One of the main points to be aware of about the striped bass is that they have a preference for specific habitats. They prefer water with moderate to high salinity, and they are more likely to gather in areas of structure, including reefs, rock or sandbars. Jetties are also popular. These structures provide shelter for the fish as well as create zones that attract baitfish. Estuaries and coves that have slow-moving waters also attract stripe bass as they provide various food items, as well as protection from predators larger than them.

Changes in the seasons affect the behaviour and lifestyle of the striped bass. In summer the striped bass can be located in deeper waters near the coast. They consume menhaden, herring and various baitfish. In the winter and fall seasons, the striped bass migrate closer to shores, and then into rivers in order to begin spawning. It is the best time to catch the striped bass as they are more aggressive and eat a lot to prepare to spawn.

In the search for stripe bass, it is essential to keep an eye on the time of day and the tide cycle. Striped bass can be found most active in low-light conditions like dawn and sunset. At daytime they will seek deep waters or regions covered in vegetation, like the outcrops of rocky wrecks. When the tide shifts and the water temperature rises, striped bass are more likely to relocate to areas that have stronger flow, which means they will are more likely to have a better time getting their prey.

The diet and habits of striped bass can be crucial when trying to capture the fish. They feed on many different prey species comprising baitfish, such as herring, sand eels and menhaden, aswell being crabs, shrimp and the squid. Being aware of what the striped bass that are in your region are eating can provide you with an edge when picking the appropriate bait or lure to choose.

Alongside understanding the habits and habitat of the striped bass, it's crucial to understand local regulations regarding the capture and released. There are many areas with bag sizes and limits along with limitations on the times and places it is possible to fish for stripe bass, especially during the spawning period. It is essential to adhere to these guidelines to ensure long-term viability of the population of striped bass.

Understanding the environment and behavior of striped bass are essential in becoming an effective angler. When you are aware of the time of the day, tide cycles and the preferred habitats for the striped bass and also their eating habits and patterns for migration You can increase the odds of catching this rare fish. Make sure you practice safe methods of fishing and adhere to local laws to ensure long-term health of the population of striped bass.

## Chapter 25: Methods Of The Capture Of Striped Bass From Land

Casting a line for striped bass along the shore is an enjoyable and satisfying experience. If you're casting off the beach or wading through the waters of shallow depth there are some methods that will aid you in catching more bass.

The most crucial points to remember while fishing from shore for Striped bass is to look over the water and surroundings. Watch for indications of activity from fish including birds diving or baitfish soaring into the lake. Striped bass tend to be located near structures, including jetties, sandbars or areas of sand. They can also change direction according to the tide. Therefore, planning your fishing excursions around the tides at low or high can prove beneficial.

Another important element of fishing from shore is the choice of the baits or lures you use. Striped bass are known for their ability to be omnivorous eaters, which is why it is important to choose a bait which will tempt them to catch. One popular option is to use baits that are local to the area including clams Sandworms, or eels. Also, you can try lures that mimic movements of baitfish such as soft plastics, jigs and even swimbaits. Whichever option you pick be sure that you make sure to match the size and colors of your lures or baits to the conditions in which you are fishing.

When you've picked the bait or lure after which it's time to set your line. If you're fishing from shore usually, you'll use spinning rods with reels combination. Be sure to place yourself in an area that offers enough room to cast casting that is long and precise. In order to increase the chances of success, cast along the shore or in areas that have the structure. Take note of the direction of tide, too. casting along the tide could aid your lure or bait to flow more easily within the ocean.

If you experience the bite, it's crucial to act quickly and calmly. Stripers are known to be tough fighters. You'll need to ensure that the drag is properly set prior to reeling in the line. Maintain a steady grip on your rod, and slowly reel it in by pumping the rod to draw the fish closer to the shore. If the fish seems particularly robust, you might need to move yourself closer to the shoreline to achieve an improved angle. However, whatever you do, you shouldn't push or drag the fish towards shore. This could result in your line snapping or the fish fleeing.

If you've successfully caught the striped bass you've been hunting for It is important to treat the fish with care and reverence. If you're planning to keep the fish, ensure that you kill it swiftly as well as humanely. If you're planning to release the fish, ensure to wash your hands with soap or utilize a dehooking tool to gently remove the hook. Keep the fish in a horizontal position within the water until at the point of release and ensure that it has recovered its strength and can swim out independently.

The fishing on shore for striped bass is a memorable adventure. When you are able to observe the water and deciding on the best lures and baits, and employing the right fishing and casting methods and techniques, you'll be in the process of catching many more fish off the shore. Be sure to exercise responsible stewardship and take responsibility to hold and let go of any fish that you capture with care and respect.

www.ingramcontent.com/pod-product-compliance
Lightning Source LLC
Chambersburg PA
CBHW051725020426
42333CB00014B/1156